GCSE Maths is Easy

Higher Tier

For the Grade 9-1 Exams

www.How2Become.com

As part of this product you have also received FREE access to online tests that will help you to pass GCSE Maths assessments.

To gain access, simply go to:

www.MyEducationalTests.co.uk

Get more products for passing any test at:

www.How2Become.com

Orders: Please contact How2Become Ltd, Suite 1, 60 Churchill Square Business Centre, Kings Hill, Kent ME19 4YU.

You can order through Amazon.co.uk under ISBN: 9781912370528, via the website www.How2Become.com or through Gardners.com.

ISBN: 9781912370528

First published in 2018 by How2Become Ltd.

Typeset by Katie Noakes for How2Become Ltd.

Disclaimer

Every effort has been made to ensure that the information contained within this guide is accurate at the time of publication. How2Become Ltd is not responsible for anyone failing any part of any selection process as a result of the information contained within this guide. How2Become Ltd and their authors cannot accept any responsibility for any errors or omissions within this guide, however caused. No responsibility for loss or damage occasioned by any person acting, or refraining from action, as a result of the material in this publication can be accepted by How2Become Ltd.

The information within this guide does not represent the views of any third party service or organisation.

CONTENTS

HOW TO USE THIS GUIDE

HOW TO USE THIS GUIDE

Welcome to *GCSE Maths is Easy* – the complete guide to complement your GCSE mathematical learning. This guide can be used alongside the new national curriculum which ensures you are fully prepared for your GCSE exams.

Within this guide, we have done our best to breakdown the national curriculum in clear, easy-to-read chapters. The book will be broken down into six main chapters:

- Numbers;

- Ratio, Proportion, and Rates of Change;

- Geometry and Measures;

- Probability and Statistics;

- Algebra;

- Problem Solving.

Within each of these chapters, content will broken down into smaller, more manageable chunks. This will allow you to revise specific sections, as well as work through sections that you might have forgotten about.

Outlined below aresome of the main areas that will be covered during this guide:

Whole Numbers	Decimals	Fractions	Percentages
Approximation	Multiples	Factors	Indices
Standard Form	Surds	Finances	Ratio

Percentages	Direct / Inverse Proportion	Angles and Lines	2D and 3D Shapes
Circles	Sectors	Transfor-mations	Pythagoras' Theorem
Units of Measure	Trigonometry	Vectors	Probability
Collecting Data	Analysing Data	Algebraic Expressions	Linear Equations
Simultaneous Equations	Quadratic Equations	Inequalities	Sequences
Graphs	Transfor-mations of Curves	Algebraic Fractions	Problem Solving

Our advice when working through this guide is to work through the content in which it appears in the book. We have carefully laid out this book so that you learn the very basics, before attempting more complicated maths.

WHY SHOULD I USE THIS BOOK?

This GCSE revision book is like no other. Yes, it's packed full of knowledge and sample questions, and yes, it covers the entire national curriculum, but what makes this book truly remarkable is its ability to put 'fun' into it. In other words, we have created our book with the intention to use interesting knowledge, real-life events, and random facts to assist your learning, making it easier to remember!

Good luck and we wish you all the best.

The how2become team

The How2Become Team

CHAPTER 1
NUMBERS

In this chapter, we will take a look at the following areas:

- BIDMAS;

- Whole Numbers;

- Decimals, Fractions, and Percentages;

- Approximation;

- Multiples and Factors;

- Indices;

- Standard Form;

- Surds;

- Finances.

B.I.D.M.A.S

BIDMAS is an acrostic which can be used to remember how you should go about solving maths questions.

BIDMAS is a great way to remember which order you should work out operations, in a calculation that has more than one operation.

The order of operations is as follows:

Brackets ( )

Indices X^2

Division ÷

Multiplication ×

Addition +

Subtraction −

Using BIDMAS, work out the following calculation:

$$8 + 4 \times 3 - 6$$

How to work it out:

- Remember the order of operations.

- In this calculation, you have addition, multiplication and subtraction.

- To start, you should work out which operation needs to be done first. In this case, it is multiplication.

$4 \times 3 = 12$

- Next, we would do the addition.

$8 + 12 = 20$

- Finally, we would do the subtraction.

$20 - 6 = 14$

EXERCISE 1

1) The height of the world's tallest man, in centimetres, is approximately:

$22 + 500 \div 2$ 247cm

$22 + 225 = $ ✗

$22 + 250 = 272$ cm

2) The height of the world's smallest woman, in centimetres, is approximately:

$10 + (8 \times 12) - 11 \times 4$ 62cm

$10 + 96$ 44

106 − 44 = 62

°1'06
-844
62

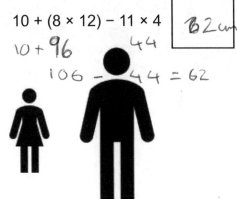

WHOLE NUMBERS

When it comes to whole numbers, you can place these digits under headings. These are called

PLACE VALUE HEADINGS.

Place value headings allow you to work out what each number represents, whether its hundreds, thousands, millions and so forth.

Below we have created the place value columns which you MUST learn.

Millions	Hundred thousands	Ten thousands	Thousands	Hundreds	Tens	Units
4	5	8	1	2	3	6

As you can see, the above number is broken down into columns. These columns help you work out what each number stands for.

Let's break this number down even further!

4 000 000 = 4 million

500 000 = 5 hundred thousand

80 000 = 80 thousand

1 000 = 1 thousand

200 = 2 hundred

30 = 3 tens (thirty)

6 = 6 units

To break down the number, begin on the right side. Moving left, put a comma after every 3 digits. This will help you to read the number.

4,581,236

So, this number is four million, five hundred and eighty one thousand, two hundred and thirty six.

INEQUALITY SYMBOLS

>	Greater than.
<	Less than.
≥	Greater than or equal to.
≤	Less than or equal to.

<u>For example:</u>

- 5,000 > 2,000 = 5,000 is GREATER THAN 2,000.

- 300 < 600 = 300 is LESS THAN 600.

EXERCISE 2

1) Draw in the missing inequality symbol:

$$29 \quad \boxed{<} \quad 42$$

Did you know that the skull is made up of 29 bones!

2) Which is greater? <u>Circle your answer.</u>

(0.15)   0.015

3) Draw in the missing inequality symbol:

$$5.9 \quad \boxed{>} \quad 3.2$$

Did you know that the height of the Eiffel Tower changes by 5.9 inches due to temperature changes?

DECIMALS, FRACTIONS, AND PERCENTAGES

Fractions, decimals, and percentages are all ways of describing **PART** of a whole number.

You can convert between fractions, decimals, and percentages, and you need to learn how to do this!

FRACTION	DECIMAL	PERCENTAGE
$^1/_2$	0.5	50%
$^1/_4$	0.25	25%
$^3/_4$	0.75	75%
$^1/_3$	0.3333...	33 $^1/_3$%
$^2/_3$	0.6666...	66 $^2/_3$%
$^1/_5$	0.2	20%
$^2/_5$	0.4	40%
$^1/_{10}$	0.1	10%
$^2/_{10}$	0.2	20%

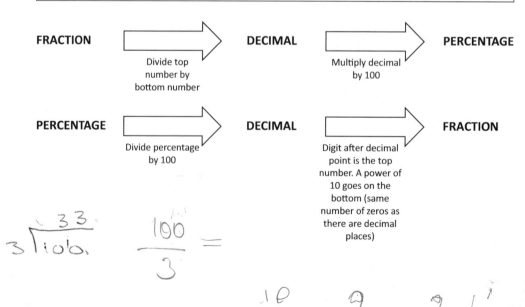

FRACTION ⟹ DECIMAL
Divide top number by bottom number

DECIMAL ⟹ PERCENTAGE
Multiply decimal by 100

PERCENTAGE ⟹ DECIMAL
Divide percentage by 100

DECIMAL ⟹ FRACTION
Digit after decimal point is the top number. A power of 10 goes on the bottom (same number of zeros as there are decimal places)

FRACTIONS

A fraction is **PART** of a whole number.

A **FRACTION** is made up of 2 numbers.

$\dfrac{2}{5}$ ⟶ The top number is called the NUMERATOR.
⟶ The bottom number is called the DENOMINATOR.

THE NUMERATOR

The numerator number tells you how many parts are taken.

THE DENOMINATOR

The denominator number tells you how many equal parts there are 'altogether'.

$\dfrac{1}{1}$ $\dfrac{1}{2}$ $\dfrac{1}{2}$ $\dfrac{1}{3}$ $\dfrac{1}{3}$ $\dfrac{1}{3}$ $\dfrac{1}{4}$ $\dfrac{1}{4}$ $\dfrac{1}{4}$ $\dfrac{1}{4}$

EQUIVALENT FRACTIONS

Equivalent = 'the same as'.

Equivalent fractions look different, but are actually representing the same thing.

$\dfrac{1}{2}$

$\dfrac{2}{4}$

$\dfrac{4}{8}$

As you can see, the above fraction bars demonstrate the same amount being shaded in, but they are just written in a different way. Obviously $\frac{1}{2}$ is easier to understand than $\frac{4}{8}$, but they do mean the same thing!

You can make equivalent fractions by multiplying or dividing the top AND bottom number, by the SAME number.

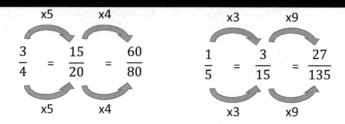

SIMPLIFYING FRACTIONS

The word **SIMPLIFYING** simply means 'to make it simple'. Sometimes, you can simplify fractions in order to make them easier to understand.

This is similar to finding equivalent fractions. However, instead of multiplying, you will divide – you want to make the fraction smaller!

To simplify fractions, you will need to divide the top AND bottom number, by the SAME number.

$$\frac{60}{80} \overset{\div4}{\underset{\div4}{=}} \frac{15}{20} \overset{\div5}{\underset{\div5}{=}} \frac{3}{4} \qquad \frac{27}{135} \overset{\div9}{\underset{\div9}{=}} \frac{3}{15} \overset{\div3}{\underset{\div3}{=}} \frac{1}{5}$$

• To work out whether a fraction is in its simplest form, you will need to keep dividing, until no number is able to be divided into both the top and bottom number of the fraction.

ORDERING FRACTIONS

In order to work out which fraction is bigger or smaller, you will need to make the bottom numbers of the fraction the same. Remember, whatever you do to the bottom number, you must do to the top.

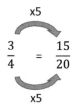
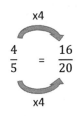

$$\frac{3}{4} \overset{x5}{\underset{x5}{=}} \frac{15}{20} \qquad \frac{4}{5} \overset{x4}{\underset{x4}{=}} \frac{16}{20}$$

1) Find a number that both 4 and 5 go into = 20.
2) Because you've changed the bottom number, you need to multiply the top number by however many it took to reach 20.
3) So $\frac{4}{5}$ is bigger than $\frac{3}{4}$.

MIXED AND IMPROPER FRACTIONS

MIXED FRACTIONS have both an integer and a fraction.

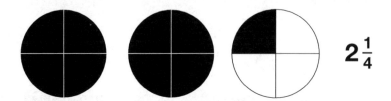

$$2\frac{1}{4}$$

An IMPROPER FRACTION is where the top number of the fraction is bigger than the bottom number of the fraction.

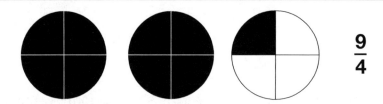

$$\frac{9}{4}$$

To write a mixed fraction as an improper fraction:	To write an improper fraction as a mixed fraction:
$4\frac{2}{3}$	$\dfrac{16}{5}$
• Multiply the whole number by the bottom number of the fraction (12). Add the top number of the fraction (12 + 2 = 14). • This number will form the top part of the fraction. • Leave the bottom number of the fraction as it is: $\dfrac{14}{3}$	• How many 5s go into 16 exactly? Answer = 3 • How many are left over? Answer = 1 • So, 3 is the whole number. • 1 is the top part of the fraction, and the bottom number will be the same: $3\frac{1}{5}$

ADDING AND SUBTRACTING FRACTIONS *

CROSSBOW METHOD

$$\frac{3}{4} + \frac{2}{5} = \frac{15+8}{20} = \frac{23}{20} = 1\frac{3}{20}$$

Draw two diagonal lines through both of the fractions as shown. (This forms the **CROSS** which looks like a multiplication sign).

It tells you to multiply the 3 by 5 = 15
It tells you to multiply the 4 by 2 = 8.

Then draw your **BOW** (from the bottom number of the first fraction to the bottom number of the second fraction).

Multiply these two numbers: 4 × 5 = 20

Add the numerator numbers together and convert your fraction to a proper fraction.

$$\frac{4}{7} - \frac{1}{3} = \frac{12-7}{21} = \frac{5}{21}$$

Draw two diagonal lines through both of the fractions as shown. (This forms the **CROSS** which looks like a multiplication sign).

It tells you to multiply the 4 by 3 = 12
It tells you to multiply the 7 by 1 = 7.
12 − 7 = 5

Then draw your **BOW** (from the bottom number of the first fraction to the bottom number of the second fraction).

Again, multiply these two numbers: 7 × 3 = 21

Now minus 7 from 12 to complete the answer.

MULTIPLYING AND DIVIDING FRACTIONS

ARROW METHOD

$$\frac{5}{9} \times \frac{3}{5} = \frac{15}{45} = \frac{3}{9} = \frac{1}{3}$$

Draw an arrow through the two top numbers and multiply.
5 × 3 = 15

Draw an arrow through the two bottom numbers.
9 × 5 = 45

Done! (Some fractions will be able to be simplified, as shown in the above example).

$$\frac{4}{7} \div \frac{3}{4} = \frac{4}{7} \times \frac{4}{3} = \frac{16}{21}$$

This is actually quite simple. Turn the second fraction upside down. Change the divide sum to a multiply, and then use the **SAME** method as if you were multiplying.

You will get the answer correct every time!

Key thing to remember:

When you are dividing two fractions, don't forget to turn the second fraction **UPSIDE DOWN** before you multiply the numbers.

WORK OUT A FRACTION OF A NUMBER

To find a fraction of something:

1) Divide the whole number by the bottom number of the fraction.

2) Then, multiply by the top number of the fraction.

Alternatively:

1) Multiply the whole number by the top number of the fraction.

2) Then, divide the number by the bottom number of the fraction.

EXAMPLE

Work out $\frac{5}{8}$ of £272.

STEP 1

Divide 272 by the bottom number of the fraction (8).

- $272 \div 8 = 34$ - this is $\frac{1}{8}$

STEP 2

Multiply 34 by the top number of the fraction (5).

- $34 \times 5 = £170.$

So, $\frac{5}{8}$ of £272 is £170.

ACTIVITY TIME!

Work out the following:

$\frac{11}{20}$ of £880 $\frac{3}{4}$ of 1,428 $\frac{6}{11}$ of 990

DECIMALS

Like fractions, decimals are another way of writing a number that is not whole.

A decimal is in fact 'in-between numbers'.

6.48 ⟶ This is in between the number 6 and the number 7.

USING PLACE VALUES

In order to work out what the decimal is representing, you should use place values.

These include: units, tenths, hundredths and thousandths.

ADDING AND SUBTRACTING DECIMALS

0.5 + 0.62

How to work it out:

$$+\begin{array}{r} 0.5 \\ 0.62 \\ \hline 1.12 \end{array}$$

The decimal points need to be lined up!

Your answer should begin by adding the decimal point in first, and then add up the columns from right to left.

2.46 − 1.35

How to work it out:

```
  2.46
- 1.35
  ────
  1.11
```

The decimal points need to be lined up!

Your answer should begin by adding the decimal point in first, and then subtracting the columns from right to left.

MULTIPLYING AND DIVIDING DECIMALS

2.5 × 0.2

How to work it out:

- Remove the decimal points.

  25 × 2 = 50

- Now add in the decimal points. **REMEMBER**, you need to work out how many numbers come **AFTER** the decimal point in the question.

- You should notice that two numbers come after the decimal point (the .5 and the .2).

- Therefore 2 numbers need to come after the decimal point in the answer.

  25 × 2 = .50

- So the answer would be 0.50 or 0.5. It is usually written 0.5 (the 0 at the end is not necessary).

REMEMBER: division is easy if you are dividing by whole numbers. You need to move the decimal points in both numbers the same number of places.

5.39 ÷ 1.1

How to work it out:

Move the decimal point 1 space.

53.9 ÷ 11.

*   Now ignore the decimal point in 53.9, do long division and then add it in at the end.

$$\begin{array}{r} 049 \\ 11\overline{)539} \\ 5 \\ 0 \\ \overline{53} \\ 44 \\ \overline{99} \\ 99 \\ \overline{0} \end{array}$$

Put the decimal point in the answer directly above the decimal point in the question.

ANSWER = $11\overline{)53.9}^{04.9}$

RECURRING DECIMALS

A recurring decimal is a decimal that goes on forever. For example, 0.4̇ means 0.444444.....

If two dots are used, this shows the beginning and the end of the recurring numbers. For example 0.6̇13̇ means 0.613613613...

PERCENTAGES

Percentages are used to work out part of a number. For example 25% of something is equivalent to $\frac{1}{4}$ or 0.25

Percent ⟶ out of 100

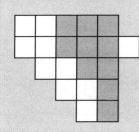

- To work out what percentage of this shape is shaded, you first need to work out the total number of squares.

Total number of squares = 20.

- Now work out the number of squares shaded.

Number of squares shaded = 10.

- There are 20 equal parts which means each square represents 5% (100 ÷ 20 = 5). So, 5% × 10 (shaded squares) = 50%

FIND X% OF Y

To work out the percentage of a number, i.e. 35% of 300, you should **ALWAYS** use the following method, as it guarantees that you get the correct answer.

35% of 300

Step 1 = 300 ÷ 100 = 3

Step 2 = 3 × 35 = 105.

Step 3 = 105 is 35% of 300.

Alternatively, you can convert the percentage into a decimal. So 35% becomes 0.35 × 300 = 105.

EXPRESSING X AS A PERCENTAGE OF Y

To express a number as a percentage of something else, you will need to divide x by y and then multiply by 100.

Write 30p as a percentage of £1.20

Step 1

Convert the pounds into pence. You need to work with the same units. £1.20 = 120p.

Step 2

Divide 30p by 120p.

$30 \div 120 = 0.25$

Step 3

Multiply this by 100.

$0.25 \times 100 = 25\%$

ACTIVITY TIME!

Work out the following:

- What is 75% of £900?

- Express 98p as a percentage of £3.50.

- What is 125% of 1,200?

- There are 118 students in Geography, 100 are non-US students. What percentage are non-US students?

EXERCISE 3

1) Match the boxes from the top row to the bottom row that have the same value. <u>The first one has been done for you.</u>

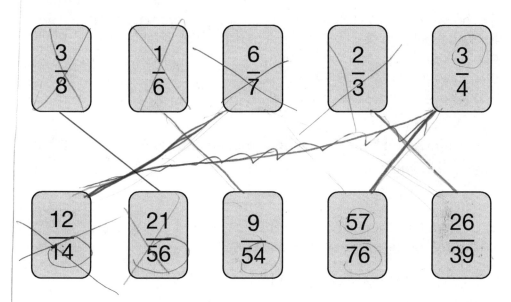

2) Work out the following:

$$12.76 \div 29 = 0.44 \checkmark$$

Did you know that the answer to this question is the size of the world's smallest country in square kilometres?

3) Work out the following:

$$70\% \text{ of } 5{,}670?$$

3969 ✓

4) **Emperor penguins live in an environment where winds speeds can reach up to** ___89___ **(mph).**

One third of 267

$$\begin{array}{r} 89 \\ 3\overline{)267} \end{array} \checkmark$$

5) Rattlesnakes are hard to kill. Even if you chop one's head off, it could still bite you $\frac{1}{6}$ of an hour plus $\frac{1}{5}$ of an hour later. How long is this?

$10 \quad + \quad 12$

(22) ✓

Fact!

6) The world's strongest man can lift 445 kilograms off the floor. It has been calculated that a gorilla could lift at least $\frac{1}{5}$ of a tonne plus $\frac{1}{2}$ a tonne. A tonne is 1,000 kilograms. How many kilograms could a gorilla lift?

$200 + 500 = 700 \text{ kg}$ ✓

$5\overline{)1000}$ 200

Fact!

7) The number of bones in the adult human body is $\frac{2}{5}$ of 515. How many bones is that?

206 bones ✓

$5\overline{)515}$ 103

202

Fact!

8) Oysters have been known to live for $\frac{5}{9}$ of 144 years. How long have oysters been know to live for?

80 years ✓ $9\overline{)144}$ 16

$\begin{array}{r} 16 \\ \times\ 5 \\ \hline 80 \end{array}$

Fact!

9) The Death Cap is a poisonous toadstool. $\frac{5}{7}$ of 42 grams of poison is enough to kill someone. How many grams is this?

30g ✓

Fact!

10) One day on the planet Mercury is much longer than a day on Earth.   One Mercury day is $\frac{1}{5}$ of 295 Earth days. How many Earth days is this?

59 days ✓ $5\overline{)295}$ 59

Fact!

11) It would take a snail about 8% of 25 weeks to crawl a mile. How long is this?

Fact!

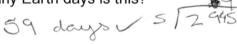

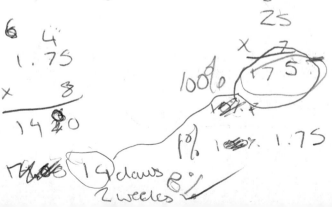

3
25

$\times\ \begin{array}{r} 4 \\ 1.75 \\ \times\ \ \ 8 \\ \hline 1420 \end{array}$

100%   175

1%   1.75

2 weeks   8%

ROUNDING UP OR ROUNDING DOWN

It is important that you know how to correctly round numbers up and down.

When the units are LESS THAN 5, you will round down.

When the units are MORE THAN 5, you will round up.

If the unit IS 5, you will round up!

There are different ways you could be asked to round a number up or down. This is usually asked by using the words 'to the nearest'.

To the nearest **ten** (10)	To the nearest **hundred** (100)	To the nearest **thousand** (1,000)
To the nearest **ten thousand** (10,000)	To the nearest **hundred thousand** (100,000)	To the nearest **million** (1,000,000)
	To the nearest **whole number**	

EXAMPLE

Round 3,449 to the nearest thousand.

Step 1 = look at the hundreds digit = '4'.

Step 2 = work out whether the last digit is between 1 and 4, or 5 and 9.

Step 3 = you should know to round the number down because '4' is between 1 and 4.

Step 4 = so, 3,449 to the nearest thousand = 3,000.

Sometimes, you will be asked to round a number to a given number of decimal places (d.p.)

The KEY thing to remember when rounding up a number to so many decimal places, is to look at the next number after the decimal place.

How to round a number to a decimal place:

STEP 1

Identify the number of decimal places you are trying to work out. For example, for 2 d.p. you will need to look at the second number **AFTER** the decimal point.

STEP 2

Then, look at the next digit to the right of this number. This is called the **DECIDER**.

- If it's 5 or higher, you will round up.

- If it's 4 or less, you will leave the number as it is.

EXAMPLE

Work out what 69.659 is to 2 d.p.

Step 1 = Identify the number of decimal places (2). So, the second number after the decimal point is 5.

Step 2 = Next, identify the decider (the next number) which is 9. Because '9' is higher than 5, this means we must round up!

Step 3 = So, to 2 d.p. this number would be 69.66

ROUNDING TO SIGNIFICANT FIGURES (S.F.)

Sometimes, you will be asked to round a number to a significant figure. This is very similar to rounding to decimal places, except that you will focus on the number.

How to round a number to significant figures:

STEP 1

Identify the number of significant figures you are working with. For example, if you are trying to work out 2 s.f. then you will focus on the **SECOND** digit.

STEP 2

Then, look at the next digit to the right of this number. This is called the **DECIDER**.

- If it's 5 or higher, you will round up.
- If it's 4 or less, you will leave the number as it is.

STEP 3

Once you have rounded the number, you should fill the gaps to complete the number (zeros will be needed up to the decimal point).

EXAMPLE

Work out 2368.52 to 3 s.f.

Step 1 = identify the number of significant figures (3). So, the third number is (6).

Step 2 = next, identify the decider (the next number) which is 8. Because '8' is higher than 5, this means we must round up!

Step 3 = So, to 3 s.f. the number would be 2370

ESTIMATING AND GUESSWORK

Sometimes, you won't be asked to work out the ACTUAL answer, and instead might be asked to ESTIMATE the answer.

To estimate:

STEP 1

Round everything off. This is your chance to simplify the calculation. For example, you may wish to round everything off to 1 s.f. Alternatively, to make it easier, you can round all the numbers to the nearest 10

STEP 2

Next, you can do the calculation. Be sure to show all of your working out. This way, the examiner is able to see your thought

EXAMPLE

Estimate the value of $\dfrac{78.8 \times 12}{18}$

KNOW THE SYMBOL!

$\approx$ means 'almost equal to'.

STEP 1

Round all the numbers to the nearest 10 = $\dfrac{80 \times 10}{20}$

STEP 2

Work out the calculation = $80 \times 10 \approx 800$ $800 \div 20 = 40$

EXERCISE 4

1) Round:

a) 36.58 to 1 s.f.

36.6   40

b) 36.57 to 1 d.p.

36.6

c) 138.72 to 3 s.f.

139

Did you know this is the approximate height of The Great Pyramid of Giza in metres?

2) What is 98,486 to the nearest 10, 100 and 1,000?

98,490

98,500

98,000

MULTIPLES

How to find the least common multiple (lcm):

Finding the 'common' multiples of numbers means finding a number that they both have in common.

EXAMPLE

Find the lowest common multiple of 2 and 5.

Step 1

Write out the first few multiples of 2.

2, 4, 6, 8, 10…

Step 2

Write out the first few multiples of 5.

5, 10, 15, 20, 25…

Step 3

Find the lowest multiple that both 2 and 5 have in common.

Step 4

The lowest common multiple for 2 and 5 is 10. (There is no smaller number that is a multiple of 2 and 5, therefore this is the correct answer).

FACTORS

Factors are numbers that can be divided **EXACTLY** into other numbers.

EXAMPLE

Work out the factors of 60.

Step 1

What numbers can be divided into 60?

- $1 \times 60 = 60$
- $2 \times 30 = 60$
- $3 \times 20 = 60$
- $4 \times 15 = 60$
- $5 \times 12 = 60$
- $6 \times 10 = 60$

Step 2

Write out the numbers in ascending order.

So, the factors of 60 are:

1   2   3   4   5   6   10   12   15   20   30   60

How to find the highest common factor (hcf):

Finding the 'common' factor of two or more numbers means finding a number that factorises into each of those numbers.

EXAMPLE

Find the highest common factor of 12 and 30.

Step 1

Work out the factors of 12.

- 1, 2, 3, 4, 6, 12

Step 2

Work out the factors of 30.

- 1, 2, 3, 5, 6, 10 15, 30

Step 3

Look out for the common factors. What numbers occur in both sets?

- 1, 2, 3, 6

Step 4

So the highest common factor is 6.

PRIME FACTORS

EVERY number can be written as a **PRODUCT** of prime numbers.

PRODUCT = MULTIPLY or TIMES

THE FACTOR TREE
The best way to work out the prime factors of a number is via a factor tree.

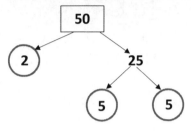

1) Find two factors to split the number (you can split the number any way you would like – you'll still end up with the same result.
2) Every time you find a prime number, circle it!
3) Keep going until you can no longer find any factors (when you're left with all prime numbers).
4) The numbers you have circled are your prime factors!

The prime factors of 50:
2 x 5 x 5

PRIME NUMBERS

Prime numbers are numbers that cannot be divided by anything else apart from the number 1 and itself.
All prime numbers up to 100 have been shaded.

1	2	3	4	5	6	7	8	9	10
11	12	13	14	15	16	17	18	19	20
21	22	23	24	25	26	27	28	29	30
31	32	33	34	35	36	37	38	39	40
41	42	43	44	45	46	47	48	49	50
51	52	53	54	55	56	57	58	59	60
61	62	63	64	65	66	67	68	69	70
71	72	73	74	75	76	77	78	79	80
81	82	83	84	85	86	87	88	89	90
91	92	93	94	95	96	97	98	99	100

<u>Always remember:</u>

1) The number 1 is **NOT** a prime number.

2) The number 2 is the **ONLY** even prime number.

3) Apart from the numbers 2 and 5, all prime numbers end in 1, 3, 7 or 9.

4) Relating back to the previous point, **NOT ALL** numbers ending in 1, 3, 7 or 9 will be prime.

HOW TO WORK OUT PRIME NUMBERS

To work out whether a number is a prime number, there are a couple of things that you can do.

1) If the number is even (2 being the exception) then you can automatically rule this out. This will not be a prime number as it will be divisible by 2.

2) Try dividing by the numbers 3 or 7. If it does divide by either of these numbers, then it is not prime. If it doesn't divide by these numbers, then it is prime. **NOTE**, this only works for prime numbers up to 120!

EXERCISE 5

1) Is the number prime? Circle yes or no.

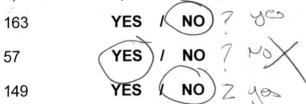

163   YES / NO ? yes

57   YES / NO ? No ✗

149   YES / NO 2 yes

2) Find the lowest common multiple for the following pairs of numbers.

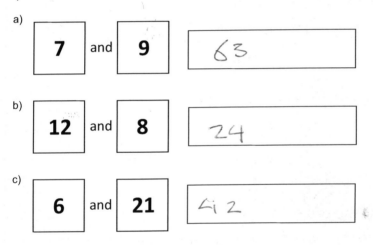

a)

| 7 | and | 9 | 63

b)

| 12 | and | 8 | 24

c)

| 6 | and | 21 | 42

3) Place the following numbers in the venn diagram.

12   8   36   40   48   84   6   2

Factors of 12   Multiples of 4

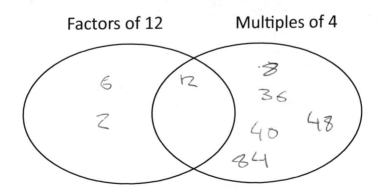

6

12   8
          36

2   40   48

          84

INDICES

Here is a number written in index form:

$$5^6$$

This is a short way of writing $5 \times 5 \times 5 \times 5 \times 5 \times 5$.

The power or index number shows how many times a number is multiplied by itself.

This can be used in algebra too:

$$A^4$$

This is a short way of writing $a \times a \times a \times a$.

Key things to remember:

- A number to the power of 0 is always 1. $(3{,}853^0 = 1)$
- A number to the power of 1 is just the number itself. $(635^1 = 635)$
- The number 1 to any power will still be 1. $(1^{312} = 1)$
- If you have a negative power, turn the number upside down, and make the negative power a positive. $(6^{-4} = \dfrac{1}{6^4} = \dfrac{1}{1296})$

If you are multiplying two numbers which contain powers, you will ADD them.

EXAMPLES

$5^2 \times 5^4 = 5^{2+4} = 5^6$

$3^5 \times 3^{-4} = 3^{5+(-4)} = 3^1$

In the second example, because we are dealing with a negative power, we subtract.

If you are dividing two numbers which contain powers, you will **SUBTRACT** them.

EXAMPLES

$5^4 \div 5^2 = 5^{4-2} = 5^2$

$3^5 \div 3^{-4} = 3^{5-(-4)} = 3^9$

In the second example, because we are subtracting a negative number, we must remember that two − change to a + sign, so therefore we will add.

If one power is raised to another, you must MULTIPLY them.

EXAMPLES

$(4^3)^2 = 4^{3 \times 2} = 4^6$

$(4^5)^{-2} = 4^{5 \times (-2)} = 4^{-10}$

In the second example, we are dealing with a raised negative number. Therefore when you multiply the numbers, the answer will be a negative raised number.

EXERCISE 6

1) Simplify the following calculations:

a) $8^6 \times 8^{10}$

8^{16}

b) $(x^6)^4$

x^{24}

c) $9^{11} \div 9^7$

9^4

d) $(8^4 \times 8^{12}) \div 8^2$

$8^{16} \div 8^2 \quad = 8^{14}$

2) Circle whether the statement is true or false.

a) A number to the power of 1 is ALWAYS 1.
   TRUE / (FALSE)

b) When you multiply, you will ADD the powers.
   (TRUE) / FALSE

c) The power of 10 means adding that many zeros.

   TRUE / (FALSE)

d) If you raise one power to another, you divide.
   TRUE / (FALSE)

STANDARD FORM

Standard form is a great way to write really LARGE or really SMALL numbers.

Number between 1 and 10   The n symbol is the number of places the decimal point moves.

Express 346,000 in standard form.

STEP 1

Move the decimal point so that the first number is between 1 and 10.

- 3.46 $(1 \leq A < 10)$

STEP 2

Count how many places the decimal point has moved = 5.

This gives us 10^5

346,000

STEP 3

So we have 3.46×10^5

Key things to remember:

- If you are dealing with a large number, the nth term with be **POSITIVE**.

- If you are dealing with a small number, the nth term with be **NEGATIVE**.

- If you are asked to work out a calculation which contains standard form, you will need to first work out the number, and then do the calculation.

- If you are asked to write out numbers from smallest to biggest, you will need to make sure all of the numbers are written in standard form. Next you will group the numbers with the same **POWER**, and order them accordingly. Lastly, arrange the groups of numbers based on the front number.

$$3.4 \quad \text{x} \quad 10^3 \qquad = \qquad 3400$$

$$5.6 \quad \text{x} \quad 10^{-4} \qquad = \qquad 0.00056$$

Interesting Facts!

1) The first number ALWAYS has to be between 1 and 10.

2) The nth power (the n sign next to the 10) is based on how many places the decimal point moves.

3) The nth power is POSITIVE for big numbers, and NEGATIVE for small numbers.

EXERCISE 7

1) Arrange these numbers in order from smallest to biggest.

$$3.35 \times 10^5 \qquad 6.34 \times 10^{-3} \qquad 5530 \qquad 0.00035$$

4   2   3   1

2) Change this number from its standard index form to its actual number.

$$0.0000\, 7.79 \times 10^{-4}$$

0.000779

3) Change this number from its standard index form to its actual number.

$$1.43 \times 10^3$$

1430.

4) Change this number from its standard index form to its actual number.

$$1.6 \times 10^3 \qquad 1600$$

Did you know that this is approximately the weight (in lbs) of a fully grown polar bear?

Fact!

SURDS

A surd is an expression that uses a root symbol, for example a square root($\sqrt{\ }$) or cubed root($^3\sqrt{\ }$), to write an irrational number.

Surds are used for accuracy as irrational numbers cannot be written precisely as they do not recur or terminate.

EXAMPLE $\sqrt{16} = 4$ is NOT a surd

$\sqrt{8} = 2.828427\ldots$ IS a surd

For GCSE Maths, you need to be able to simplify surds.

$$\sqrt{ab} = \sqrt{a} \times \sqrt{b}$$

$$\sqrt{24} = \sqrt{4} \times \sqrt{6}$$

$$\sqrt{24} = 2\sqrt{6}$$

$$\sqrt{a} \times \sqrt{a} = a$$

$$\sqrt{15} \times \sqrt{5} = \sqrt{75}$$

$$\sqrt{75} = \sqrt{25} \times \sqrt{3}$$

$$\sqrt{75} = 5\sqrt{3}$$

$$\frac{\sqrt{a}}{\sqrt{b}} = \sqrt{\frac{a}{b}} = \sqrt{a \div b}$$

$$\frac{\sqrt{24}}{\sqrt{12}} = \sqrt{\frac{24}{12}} = \sqrt{24 \div 12} = \sqrt{2}$$

EXERCISE 8

1) Simplify: $\sqrt{3} \times \sqrt{12}$

$\sqrt{3} \times \sqrt{12} = \sqrt{36} = 6$

2) Simplify: $\sqrt{\dfrac{16}{8}}$

$\sqrt{2}$

3) Simplify: $2\sqrt{5} \times 3\sqrt{5}$

30

4) Simplify: $\sqrt{12 \div 8}$

$\sqrt{\dfrac{3}{2}}$

FINANCES

Finances are important for not only your exams, but for the real world, too!

SALARY

When you go to work, you will be paid a salary. A salary is the amount of money you earn, usually over the course of a year.

For example:

If you earned a salary of £30,000 per year, your monthly pay would be 30,000 ÷ 12 = £2,500. This is the **gross pay**.

The gross pay is the amount of money **BEFORE** deductions.

The net pay is what's left **AFTER** deductions are made.

Deductions will include tax and National Insurance. It could also include any Pension Scheme Contribution.

NI

Two words that you should bear in mind are **INCREASE** and **DECREASE**.

- An increase is additional money. I.e. making a profit.
- A decrease is a reduction in money. I.e. a loss.

PERCENTAGE INCREASE AND PERCENTAGE DECREASE

To work out the percentage increase of a set of data, you need to remember this formula:

PERCENT INCREASE % = DIFFERENCE ÷ ORIGINAL NUMBER × 100

To work out the percentage decrease of a set of data, you need to remember this formula:

PERCENT DECREASE % = DIFFERENCE ÷ ORIGINAL NUMBER × 100

VAT

VAT (Value Added Tax) is paid to the government. VAT is added to items that you buy, except for things that are deemed essential, such as food.

As it currently stands, the VAT is set at 20%.

For example:

A van costs £8,000, without tax. Including tax, what is the total cost of the van?

- 8,000 ÷ 100 × 120% = £9,600

Interesting Facts!

1. Gingerbread men are classified differently with regards to VAT. If a gingerbread man has two chocolate spots for eyes, then there is NO VAT. Any other chocolate decorations, and VAT applies.

2. The Jaffa Cake fiasco — because this is deemed as a cake, and not a biscuit, VAT is NOT applied!

EXERCISE 9

1. Michael is saving money to buy his first house. Currently, Michael has £3,800 in his bank account. His bank account pays 5% interest each year. How much money will Michael have after the first year?

£3990 ✓

2. In April, John earned £2,870. On his payslip, it shows that John was taxed £574. What percentage rate of tax did John pay?

20% ✓

3. Michael wants to buy a new house. The house he is looking at is currently £320,000. The house market is set to drop its prices in the next month. Michael has a limit of £102,400. By what percentage does the house market need to drop its price in order for Michael to be able to afford the house?

68% ✓

4. The following table shows the prices of a travel agents prices for holidays for next year.

HOLIDAY PRICES				
Types of Holiday Deals	Turkey	Mexico	America	Spain
All inclusive	£276pp	£720pp	£880pp	£320pp
Half board	£220pp	£640pp	£795pp	£275pp
Self-Catering	£180pp	£550pp	£620pp	£235pp

How much would it cost for a family of five to book a holiday, all inclusive, to America? They have a 20% discount voucher on the total price.

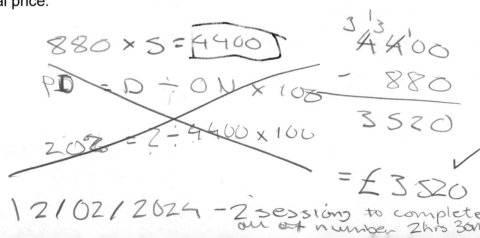

$880 \times 5 = \boxed{4400}$

$\overset{3}{\cancel{4}}\overset{13}{\cancel{4}}00$
$- \quad 880$
$\overline{3520}$

$= £3520$ ✓

PD = D ÷ ON × 108

20% = ? ÷ 4400 × 100

12/02/2024 – 2 sessions to complete.
our of number 2hrs 30min

ANSWERS TO CHAPTER 1

EXERCISE I

1) 272 cm

EXPLANATION:

- $500 \div 2 = 250$
- $22 + 250 = 272$ cm

2) 62 cm

EXPLANATION:

- $10 + (8 \times 12) - 11 \times 4$
- $10 + 96 - 11 \times 4$
- $10 + 96 - 44$
- $106 - 44$

EXERCISE 2

1) <

EXPLANATION:

- 29 is smaller than 42. Therefore, you would write this as:

  $29 < 42$

2) 0.15

3) >

EXPLANATION:

*   5.9 is greater than 3.2. Therefore, you would write this as:

    5.9 > 3.2

EXERCISE 3

1) Your answer should look like this:

* $3/8 = {}^{21}/_{56}$

* $1/6 = {}^{9}/_{54}$

* $6/7 = {}^{12}/_{14}$

* $2/3 = {}^{26}/_{39}$

* $3/4 = {}^{57}/_{76}$

2) 0.44

EXPLANATION:

```
          00.44
      29 | 12.76
        - 0
         12
        - 0
         127
       - 116
          116
        - 116
          000
```

3) 3,969

EXPLANATION:

- 5,670 ÷ 100 = 56.7
- 56.7 × 10 = 3,969

4) 89 mph

EXPLANATION:

- 267 ÷ 3 = 89

5) 22 minutes

EXPLANATION:

- ⅙ of an hour = 10 minutes
- ⅕ of an hour = 12 minutes

6) 700 kg

EXPLANATION:

- ⅕ of a tonne = 200 kg
- ½ of a tonne = 500 kg

7) 206 bones

EXPLANATION:

- 515 ÷ 5 = 103
- 103 × 2 = 206

8) 80 years

EXPLANATION:

- $144 \div 9 = 16$
- $16 \times 5 = 80$

9) 30

EXPLANATION:

- $42 \div 7 = 6$
- $6 \times 5 = 30$

10) 59

EXPLANATION:

- $295 \div 5 = 59$

11) 2 weeks

EXPLANATION:

- $25 \div 100 = 0.25$
- $0.25 \times 8 = 2$

EXERCISE 4

1a) 40

EXPLANATION:

- To find 1 s.f. you need to look at the first number (3).
- Using the second number, this will tell you whether to round the first

number up or down. The second number is (6) which means we round up.

1b) 36.6

EXPLANATION:

- To find 1 d.p. you need to look at the first number AFTER the decimal point (5).

- The second number after the decimal point is (7) which means that we round up the (5) to a (6).

1c) 139

EXPLANATION:

- To find 3 s.f. you need to look at the first three numbers (138)

- The 4th digit is (7) which means we round up.

2) Your answer should look like this:

- 98,490 = to the nearest 10

- 98,500 = to the nearest 100

- 98,000 = to the nearest 1,000

EXERCISE 5

1) Your answer should look like this:

- 163 = YES

- 57 = NO

- 149 = YES

2a) 63

2b) 24

2c) 42

3) Your answer should look like this:

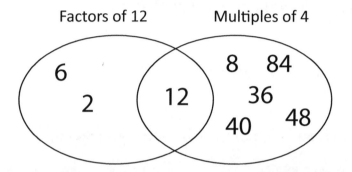

Factors of 12   Multiples of 4

6   8 84
   2   12   36
             40   48

EXERCISE 6

1a) 8¹⁶

EXPLANATION:

- When you multiply, you will need to ADD the powers.

1b) x²⁴

EXPLANATION:

- When you are raising one power to another, you will need to MULTIPLY the two powers.

1c) 9⁴

EXPLANATION:

- When you divide, you will need to SUBTRACT the two powers.

1d)8^{14}

EXPLANATION:

- $(8^{16}) \div 8^2 = 8^{14}$

2a) A number to the power of 1 is ALWAYS 1.   FALSE

2b) When you multiply, you will ADD the powers.   TRUE

2c) The power of 10 means adding that many zeros.   FALSE

2d) If you raise one power to another, you divide.   FALSE

EXERCISE 7

1) 0.00035   6.34 × 10^{-3} 5,530   3.35 × 10^5

EXPLANATION:

- 3.35 × 10^5 = 335,000
- 6.34 × 10^{-3} = 0.00634
- 5.53 × 10^3 = 5,530
- 3.5 × 10^{-4} = 0.00035
- So smallest to biggest = 0.00035   6.34 × 10^{-3} 5,530   3.35 × 10^5

2) 0.000779

3) 1,430

4) 1,600

EXERCISE 8

1)

$\sqrt{3} \times \sqrt{12}$

$\sqrt{3} \times \sqrt{12} = \sqrt{3 \times 12}$

$\sqrt{3 \times 12} = \sqrt{36}$

$\sqrt{36} = 6$

2)

$\sqrt{\dfrac{16}{8}} = \sqrt{16 \div 8}$

$\sqrt{16 \div 8} = \sqrt{2}$

3)

$2\sqrt{5} \times 3\sqrt{5} = 6\sqrt{25}$

$6\sqrt{25} = 6 \times 5$

$6 \times 5 = 30$

4)

$\sqrt{12 \div 8} = \sqrt{\dfrac{12}{8}}$

$\sqrt{\dfrac{12}{8}} = \sqrt{\dfrac{3}{2}}$

EXERCISE 9

1) £3,990

EXPLANATION:

- 3,800 ÷ 100 = 38
- 38 × 105 = 3,990

2) 20%

EXPLANATION:

- 574 ÷ 2,870 = 0.2
- 0.2 × 100 = 20%

3) 68%

EXPLANATION:

- 320,000 − 102,400 = 217,600
- 217,600 ÷ 320,000 = 0.68
- 0.68 × 100 = 68%

4) £3,520

EXPLANATION:

- 5 × 880 = £4,400
- £4,400 ÷ 100 = £44
- £44 × 20 = £880
- £4,400 - £880 = £3,520

CHAPTER 2
RATIO, PROPORTION AND RATES OF CHANGE

In this chapter, we will take a look at the following areas:

- Ratio;

- Proportion;

- Metric and Imperial Units;

- Speed, Distance, and Time;

- Scale Factor of Enlargements.

RATIO

Ratios are a way of showing how things are shared.

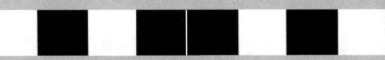

As you can see, we have 8 squares.

There are 4 white squares, and 4 black squares.

If we wanted to write this as a ratio we could write it as follows:

4 : 4

If you had a question asking what ratio of black squares there are to white squares, you would need to write the number of black squares first.

Work out the ratio of shaded squares to white squares.

Step 1

Add up the total number of squares.

• There are 24 squares in total.

Pay attention to what order you put the numbers in. The numbers must follow the order given in the question.

Step 2

Next, work out the number of shaded squares, and the number of white squares.

• There are 9 shaded squares and 15 white squares.

Therefore, the ratio of shaded squares to white squares is 9 : 15.

This can be simplified to 3 : 5.

The process of simplifying is quite easy. All you have to do is find a number that both values of the ratio can be divided by.

The ratio will be in its simplest form when there are no numbers that can be divided into both values of the ratio.

EXAMPLE

Simplify 40 : 60. Write your answer in its simplest form.

Step 1

Both '40' and '60' can be divided by 10.

- If you divide both numbers by 10, you get the ratio: 4 : 6

Step 2

Both '4' and '6' can be divided by 2.

- If you divide both numbers by 2, you would get the ratio: 2 : 3

Step 3

No other numbers can be divided equally into 2 and 3, so 2 : 3 is the simplest form of 40 : 60.

See how the ratios 40 : 60, 4 : 6 and 2 : 3 are all equivalent ratios = they all mean the same thing!

When you're working with ratios, sometimes you might be given the ratio, and then given a size of an actual part.

Your job is to work out the other size, based on the ratio given.

EXAMPLE

Jason and Matthew each have elastic bands in the ratio of 6 : 4.

If Jason has 42 elastic bands, how many elastic bands does Matthew have?

Step 1

First of all, we need to work out how the 6 (Jason) increases to 42.

6 : 4

Step 2

42 : ?

You can multiply the 6 by 7 to give you 42.

Step 3

That means we must multiply the other figure by 7 to work out how many elastic bands Matthew has.

x7   **6 : 4**   x7

42 : 28

REMEMBER

Whatever you do to one part of the ratio, has to be done to the other part of the ratio!

EXERCISE 1

1. Abbie has blue and black buttons in the ratio of 3 : 2. If there are 51 blue buttons, how many black buttons does Abbie have?

Nubla

$3\sqrt{5^2}$ $\times 2$ (34)

2. There are 600 crayons in a box. The ratio of red, blue, green and pink crayons are in the ratio of 4 : 2 : 1 : 5. If there are 100 blue crayons, work out how many red, green and pink crayons there are in the box.

$R = 200 = 4 \times 50$ $4 + 2 + 1 + 5 = 12$

$g = 50 = 1 \times 50$ $12 \times 50 = 600$

$p = 250 = 5 \times 50$

3. Below there are 10 cards. Each card has a ratio. Match the equivalent boxes from the top row to its simplest ratio in the bottom row.

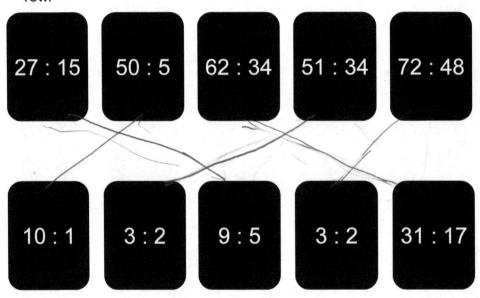

4. Simplify the following ratio:

(240 : 16)

30 : 2

15 : 1

PROPORTION

Proportional division is very simple to understand.

There are 3 steps that you need to follow in order to work out proportional division correctly.

STEP 1

Add up the two parts of the ratio.

STEP 2

Divide the total by the number of both parts (the number you get after adding both parts of the ratio).

STEP 3

Multiply that number by the number of parts you are trying to work out.

EXAMPLE

Tim and Tom are going to share £800 in the ratio of 13 : 7. How much will Tim's share be?

Step 1

Add up the ratios = 13 + 7 = 20

Step 2

Divide 800 by 20 = 800 ÷ 20 = 40

Step 3

Multiply the 40 by Tim's share (which is 13) = 40 × 13 = £520

DIRECT PROPORTION

Direct proportion is when two quantities increase or decrease in the ratio.

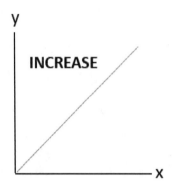

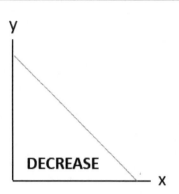

There is a direct proportion between two values if one of the values is a multiple of an another.

For example:

10 mm = 1 cm.

Direct proportion is often used to calculate the cost of petrol or exchange rates between different currencies.

The symbol for DIRECT PROPORTION is:

For example:

10 mm ∝ 1 cm

INVERSE PROPORTION

Indirect proportion is when one quantity increases as the other decreases, or vice versa.

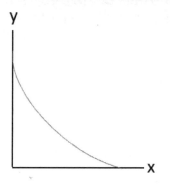

The equation for this is $y = A \div x$

The N being the number value.

<u>For example:</u>

The more workers a company has, the less time it will take to complete each task.

The symbol for INVERSE PROPORTION is:

$$b \propto \frac{1}{m}$$

EXERCISE 2

1. William has made a fruit punch. He uses three ingredients: apple juice, orange juice and cranberry juice.

   He needs to make a total of 750 ml of fruit punch. *750*

   A . O C

   If his recipe for his fruit juice is in the ratio of 11 : 8 : 6, work out how much of each ingredient he will need to make enough fruit punch.

   330 : 240 : 180

2. 4 decorators can decorate 12 rooms in one day. How many rooms could be decorated if there were 16 decorators?

   48 rooms   *48 →*

3. a is directly proportional to b. When $a = 40$ and $b = 8$.

   10   2

   a) Work out the value of a when $b = 10$.

   50 ?

   b) Work out the value of b when $a = 48$.

4. It takes 3 teachers 12 hours to mark 100 exam papers.

   How long will it take to mark 100 exam papers if 4 teachers marked the papers?   *36 hrs*   *36 ÷ 4 = 9 hrs*

5. a is inversely proportional to b^2.

   Given that $a = 4.5$ and $b = 15$:

   Find an equation for a in terms of b.

   $15^2 = 225$

Did you know that the world's biggest snow blizzard dumped around 40 inches of snow in the space of 48 hours?

Fact!

METRIC AND IMPERIAL UNITS

METRIC and IMPERIAL units are types of measurements.

METRIC UNITS	IMPERIAL UNITS
LENGTH *mm, cm, m, km*	**LENGTH** *inches, yards, feet, miles*
AREA *mm², cm², m², km²*	**AREA** *square inches, square feet, square miles*
VOLUME *mm³, cm³, m³, ml, litres*	**VOLUME** *pints, cubic inches, cubic feet, gallons*
MASS (WEIGHT) *grams, kilograms, tonnes*	**MASS (WEIGHT)** *ounces, pounds, stones, tons*
SPEED *km/h, m/s*	**SPEED** *mph*

METRIC CONVERSIONS

- 1 cm = 10 mm
- 1 m = 100 cm
- 1 km = 1000 m
- 1 kg = 1000 g
- 1 tonne = 1000 kg
- 1 litre = 1000 ml
- 1 litre = 1000 cm³
- 1 cm³ = 1 ml

Learn these off by heart!

IMPERIAL CONVERSIONS

- 1 foot = 12 inches
- 1 yard = 3 feet
- 1 gallon = 8 pints
- 1 stone = 14 pounds
- 1 pound = 16 ounces

Learn these off by heart!

CONVERSIONS!

You should try to learn as many of these as you can:

The symbol '≈' means 'approximately' or 'nearly equals to'

METRIC-IMPERIAL

- 1 inch ≈ 2.54 cm
- 1 kg ≈ 2.2 pounds
- 1 litre ≈ 1.75 pints
- 1 mile ≈ 1.6 km

IMPERIAL-METRIC

- 1 foot ≈ 30 cm
- 1 gallon ≈ 4.5 litres

HOW TO CONVERT

Step 1

Work out the **conversion factor.**

Step 2

Use the conversion factor to work out whether you need to multiply or divide.

Step 3

Do the calculation!

EXERCISE 3

1. Circle the measurement which is closest to the imperial measurement.

   a) **10 miles**   16km   1000 m   16,000 cm

   b) **12 inches**   30mm   30cm   3 m

   c) **4 pints**   2.25 l   20 l   200 ml

2. Using the following columns, place the words under the correct column. The first one has been done for you.

   ~~Kilograms~~   Litres   Metres   Grams

   Centimetres   Pounds   Kilometres   Inches

   Gallons   Stone   Millilitres   Millimetres   Tonnes

Metric Measurements	Imperial Measurements
Kilograms	

3. What is 0.8228 kilometres in metres?

Did you know that the answer to this question is the world's tallest building called Burj Khalifa?

4. Convert 380,000 centimetres in kilometres.

Did you know that the answer to this question is the world's deepest mine, located south-west of Johannesburg in South Africa?

SPEED, DISTANCE AND TIME

You need to know the relationship between speed, distance and time.

Sometimes, you will be required to work out one of the above, based on the information you are given. To do this, there is a simple formula that you **MUST** remember:

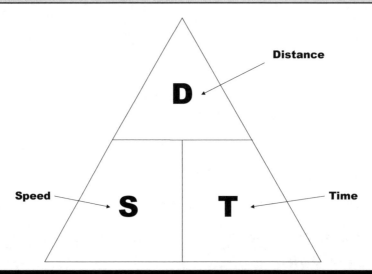

HOW TO WORK OUT SPEED

To work out the average speed, place your thumb over the speed variable ('S'), and then do the calculation.

• Speed = Distance ÷ Time

HOW TO WORK OUT DISTANCE

To work out the distance travelled, place your thumb over the distance variable ('D'), and then work out the equation.

• Distance = Speed × Time

HOW TO WORK OUT TIME

To work out the time taken, place your thumb over the time variable ('T'), and then work out the equation.

- Time = Distance ÷ Speed

EXERCISE 4

1. A lorry travels at a speed of 60 mph for 90 miles. How long will the journey take?

    1.5.hrs

2. James runs from 4.50pm until 5.20pm at an average speed of 7 km/h. How far did he go?

    3.5 km / h

3. A skier travels 1,000 metres in 100 seconds. What was the average speed of the skier?

    10 mps

Interesting Facts!

1) *Did you know that the world record for a person to solve a Rubix Cube with their feet is 25.14 seconds?*

2) *Did you know the fastest roller coaster in the United States can reach a whopping 128 mph in just 3.5 seconds?*

21 February 2024

SCALE FACTOR OF ENLARGEMENTS

Proportions can also be used to compare lengths of shapes.

In order to work out the scale factor, divide one length of the larger shape by the corresponding length on the smaller shape, this will give you the scale factor of enlargement.

You need to learn the different scale factors for length, area, and volume.

LENGTH	AREA (^{2})	VOLUME (^{3})
x2	x4	x8
x3	x9	x27

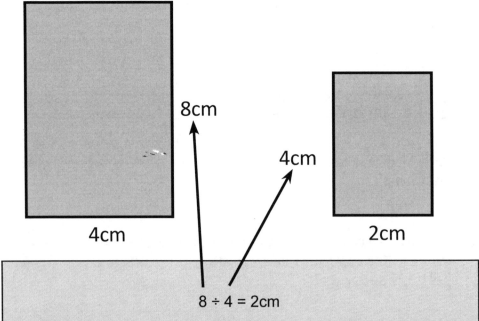

8cm

4cm

4cm

2cm

8 ÷ 4 = 2cm

- The scale factor = 2.
- The larger rectangle is twice the size of the smaller rectangle.

EXERCISE 5

1. A scale of a map is 1 cm : 30,000 km. A distance is measured as 4 cm on a map. 120,000

   How many kilometres is this equivalent based on the scale of the map?

2. The smaller cuboid is directly proportional to the larger cuboid. Work out the volume of the larger cuboid. 4.

    $192 cm^3$

   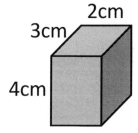

   2cm
   3cm
   4cm

   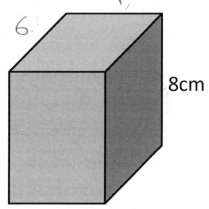 6.

   8cm

INteresting Facts!

1) **Did you know that a typical rugby pitch is 144 metres by 70 metres?**

 Fact!

2) **Did you know that a paper design of your house is called a blueprint? This uses a scale to draw your house proportionately smaller than the actual size.**

 Fact!

ANSWERS TO CHAPTER 2

EXERCISE I

1) 34

EXPLANATION:

- $51 \div 3 = 17$

- $17 \times 2 = 34$

- So there are 51 blue buttons and 34 black buttons.

2) Red = 200   Green = 50   Pink = 250

EXPLANATION:

- $600 \div 12 = 50$

- $50 \times 4 = 200$ red crayons

- $50 \times 1 = 50$ green crayons

- $50 \times 5 = 250$ pink crayons

3) Your answer should look like this:

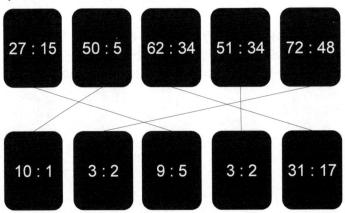

4) 15 : 1

EXPLANATION:

- Both 240 and 16 are divisible by 16.

- Therefore the ratio, in its simplest form, is 15 : 1

EXERCISE 2

1) 330 ml apple   240 ml orange   180 ml cranberry

EXPLANATION:

- $11 + 8 + 6 = 25$
- $750 \div 25 = 30$
- $30 \times 11 = 330$ apple juice
- $30 \times 8 = 240$ orange juice
- $30 \times 6 = 180$ cranberry juice

2) 48

EXPLANATION:

- $12 \div 4 = 3$
- $3 \times 16 = 48$

3a) a = 50

- ○ $40 \div 8 = 5$
- ○ $5 \times 10 = 50$

b) b = 9.6

    ○ $8 \div 40 = 0.2$

    ○ $0.2 \times 48 = 9.6$

4) 9 hours

- $3 \times 12 = 36$ hours for 1 teacher
- $36 \div 4 = 9$ hours

5) 225/b^2

EXERCISE 3

1a) 10 miles ≈ 16 km

  b) 12 inches ≈ 30 cm

  c) 4 pints ≈ 2.25 l

2) Your answer should look like this:

Metric Measurements	Imperial Measurements
Kilograms Litres Metres Grams Centimetres Kilometres Millilitres Millimetres Tonnes	Pounds Inches Gallons Stone

3) 822.8 metres

EXPLANATION:

- 0.8228 × 100 = 822.8

4) 3.8 kilometres

EXPLANATION:

- 380,000 ÷ 100,000 = 3.8

EXERCISE 4

1) 1 hour and 30 minutes

EXPLANATION:

- 90 miles divided by 60 = 1.5 hours.

2) 3.5 kilometres

EXPLANATION:

- 4.50 pm – 5.20pm = 30 minutes.
- 30 minutes = 0.5 hour.
- So, distance = 7 × 0.5 = 3.5 km.

3) 10 m/s

EXPLANATION:

- 1,000 ÷ 100 = 10 m/s

EXERCISE 5

1) 120,000 kilometres

EXPLANATION:

- $4 \times 30{,}000 = 120{,}000$ km

2) 192cm³

EXPLANATION:

- The volume of the smaller cuboid is 24cm³.

- To find the volume scale factor, you need to find the length scale factor of the cube.

- Length scale factor = 2, so the volume scale factor is $2^3 = 8$.

- Multiply the smaller cuboid of 24cm³ by 8 = 192cm³.

CHAPTER 3
GEOMETRY AND MEASURES

In this chapter, we will take a look at the following areas:

- Angles and Lines;
- 2D and 3D Shapes;
- Circles, Sectors, and Arcs;
- Transformations;
- Pythagoras' Theorem;
- Trigonometry;
- Vectors.

ANGLES

An angle is a way of measuring a turn. The size of the angle will determine the ANGLE NAME.

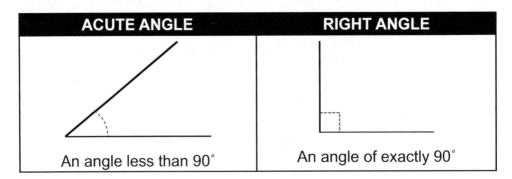

ACUTE ANGLE	RIGHT ANGLE
An angle less than 90°	An angle of exactly 90°

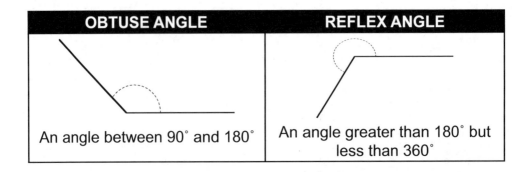

OBTUSE ANGLE	REFLEX ANGLE
An angle between 90° and 180°	An angle greater than 180° but less than 360°

These names are often used to describe triangles.

ANGLES IN A TRIANGLE

The angles in a triangle will **ALWAYS** add up to 180°.

EQUILATERAL TRIANGLE

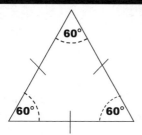

All angles are equal.

Each angle would be 60°.

ISOSCELES TRIANGLE

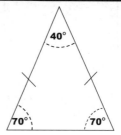

Two angles are of equal size.

SCALENE TRIANGLE

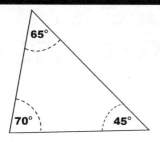

None of the angles are the same size.

RIGHT-ANGLED TRIANGLE

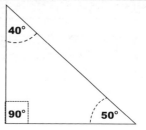

One of the angles will be 90°.

ANGLES IN A QUADRILATERAL

The angles in a quadrilateral will **ALWAYS** add up to 360°.

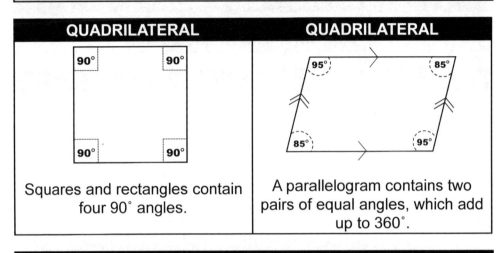

QUADRILATERAL	QUADRILATERAL
Squares and rectangles contain four 90° angles.	A parallelogram contains two pairs of equal angles, which add up to 360°.

ANGLES OF STRAIGHT LINES AND CIRCLES

The angles on a straight line will **ALWAYS** add up to 180°.

The angles in a circle will **ALWAYS** add up to 360°.

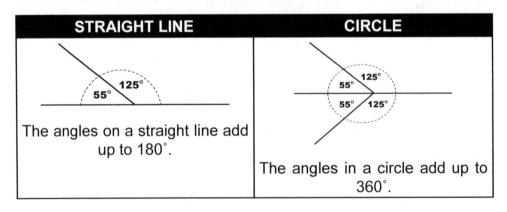

STRAIGHT LINE	CIRCLE
The angles on a straight line add up to 180°.	The angles in a circle add up to 360°.

ANGLE NOTATIONS

Sometimes, you may be asked to talk about a particular angle.

In this instance, the best way to do this is via angle notation. Angle notation uses three letters to describe which angle you are talking about.

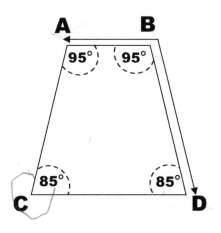

- If you are talking about angle B, you could describe the angle as **ABD** = 95°.

- If you are talking about angle C, you could describe the angle as **ACD** = 85°.

The middle letter in the notation is the actual angle, the other letters tell you which two lines join to make this angle.

EXERCISE 1

1. For the following statements, circle **true** or **false**:

   a) An isosceles triangle will always have two angles of the exact same size.

   (TRUE) / **FALSE**

   b) The angles in a circle add up to 180˚.

   TRUE / (FALSE)

   c) An obtuse angle is between 180˚ and 360˚.

   TRUE / (FALSE)

2. Calculate the size of angle **Q** in the diagram.

   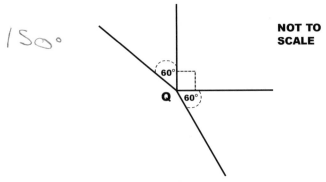

   150°

   NOT TO SCALE

3. Using a compass, draw a triangle with the angles 60°, 40° and 80°

LINES

PARALLEL LINES

Parallel lines are lines which are going in the exact same direction.

These lines NEVER touch, and are ALWAYS the same distance away from each other.

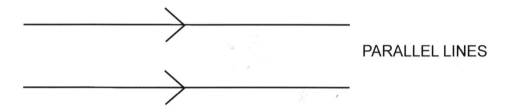

PARALLEL LINES

PERPENDICULAR LINES

Perpendicular lines are lines which meet at a right angle (90˚).

These lines ALWAYS form a 90˚ angle.

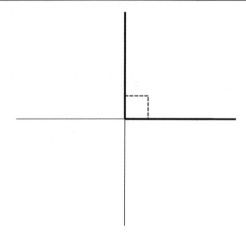

ALTERNATE 'Z' LINES

Alternate (Z) angles are always the same size.

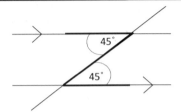

CORRESPONDING 'F' LINES

Corresponding (F) angles are always the same size.

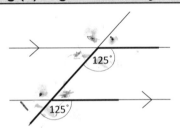

ALLIED 'C' OR 'U' LINES

ALLIED angles will add up to 180°.

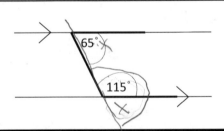 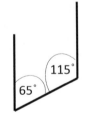

VERTICALLY OPPOSITE

VERTICALLY OPPOSITE angles are equal to one another.

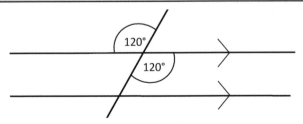

LINES OF SYMMETRY

A line of symmetry is where you can draw one (or more) lines on a shape, which act as a mirror.

Whatever is on one side of the mirror line is reflected EXACTLY the same on the other side of the mirror line.

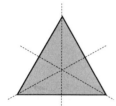 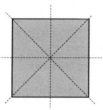 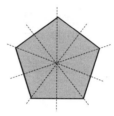 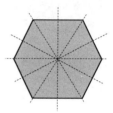

| 3 lines of symmetry | 4 lines of symmetry | 5 lines of symmetry | 6 lines of symmetry |

When working out how many lines of symmetry a shape has, remember not to count the same line twice!

ROTATIONAL SYMMETRY

Rotational symmetry is when you can rotate the whole shape, and have it still look exactly the same.

| Rotational symmetry order 1 | Rotational symmetry order 2 | Rotational symmetry order 3 | Rotational symmetry order 4 |

EXERCISE 2

1. AB and CD are parallel straight lines.

    Work out the value of *x*.

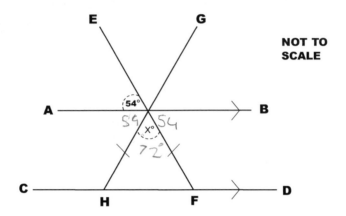

NOT TO
SCALE

2. Which lines are perpendicular?

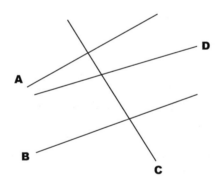

C +A

Interesting Facts!

1) Did you know that the iconic Taj Mahal was designed to be symmetrically perfect?

2) Did you know that no human has a perfectly symmetrical face?

2D SHAPES

2D shapes are shapes that only have two dimensions – length and width.

When it comes to 2D shapes, there are two types:

*   Regular polygons;

*   Irregular polygons.

REGULAR POLYGONS

TRIANGLE	NO. OF SIDES	LINES OF SYMMETRY	ROTATIONAL SYMMETRY
	• 3 sides	• 3 lines of symmetry	• Rotational symmetry of order 3

QUADRILATERAL	NO. OF SIDES	LINES OF SYMMETRY	ROTATIONAL SYMMETRY
	• 4 sides	• 4 lines of symmetry	• Rotational symmetry of order 4

PENTAGON	NO. OF SIDES	LINES OF SYMMETRY	ROTATIONAL SYMMETRY
	• 5 sides	• 5 lines of symmetry	• Rotational symmetry of order 5

HEXAGON	NO. OF SIDES	LINES OF SYMMETRY	ROTATIONAL SYMMETRY
	• 6 sides	• 6 lines of symmetry	• Rotational symmetry of order 6

HEPTAGON	NO. OF SIDES	LINES OF SYMMETRY	ROTATIONAL SYMMETRY
	• 7 sides	• 7 lines of symmetry	• Rotational symmetry of order 7

OCTAGON	NO. OF SIDES	LINES OF SYMMETRY	ROTATIONAL SYMMETRY
	• 8 sides	• 8 lines of symmetry	• Rotational symmetry of order 8

IRREGULAR POLYGONS

An irregular polygon is a shape which has different size lengths. All of its interior angles are of different size.

Let's go through some of the properties of irregular polygon shapes.

IRREGULAR TRIANGLE	IRREGULAR QUADRILATERAL	IRREGULAR PENTAGON

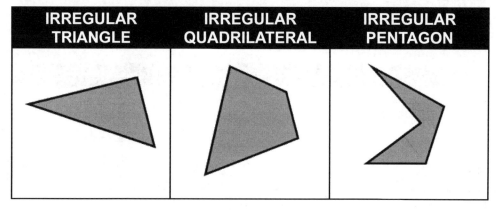

- The triangle has 3 different side lengths. Its angles would also be different.

- The quadrilateral has 4 different side lengths. Its angles would also be different.

- The pentagon has 5 different side lengths. Its angles would also be different.

IRREGULAR HEXAGON	IRREGULAR HEPTAGON	IRREGULAR OCTAGON

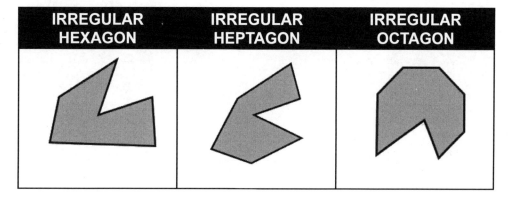

- The hexagon has 6 different side lengths. Its angles would also be different.

- The heptagon has 7 different side lengths. Its angles would also be different.

- The octagon has 8 different side lengths. Its angles would also be different.

EXERCISE 3

1. Fill in the table about shapes and sides.

Name of shape	No. of sides	Lines of symmetry
Square	4	4
Hexagon	6	6
octagon	8	8
Heptagon	7	7

2. For each of the shapes below, write whether that shape is a **regular** or **irregular** polygon.

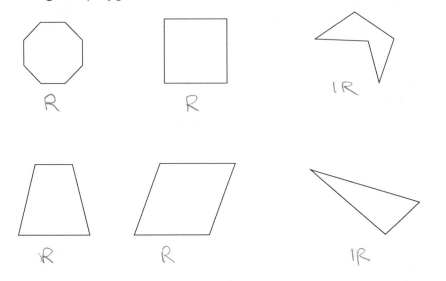

R   R   IR

R   R   IR

Interesting Fact!

1) *Did you know that the word "polygon" comes from two Greek words – 'poly' meaning 'many', and 'gon' meaning angle?*

3D SHAPES

3D shapes are SOLID shapes.

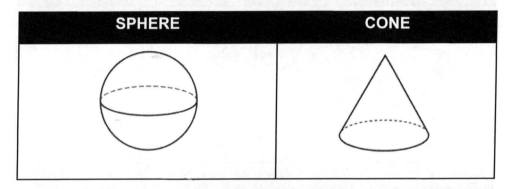

SPHERE

CONE

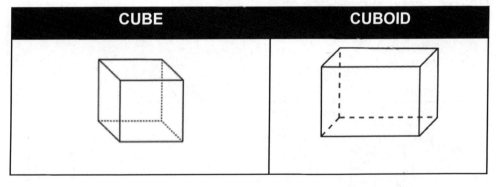

CUBE

CUBOID

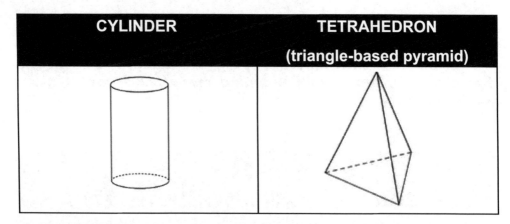

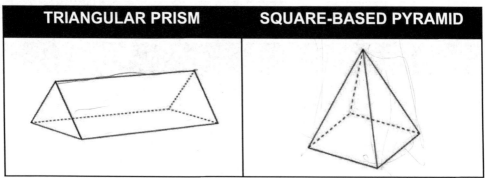

When it comes to 3D shapes, there are also some other **KEY WORDS** that you need to be aware of:

- Face;
- Vertex;
- Edge.

NETS OF 3D SHAPES

The **NET** of a shape is what the shape would look like if it was opened out flat.

There is often more than one net for each solid shape.

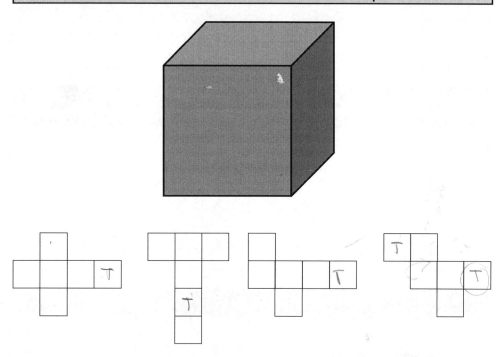

CUBOID	CUBOID NET

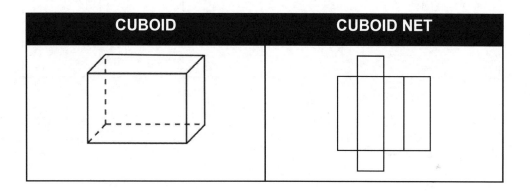

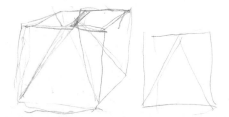

TETRAHEDRON	TETRAHEDRON NET
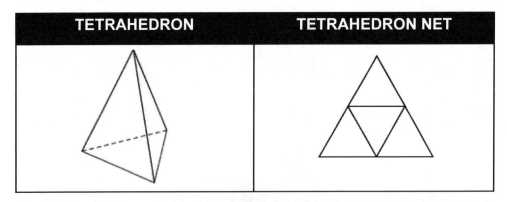

SQUARE-BASED PYRAMID	SQUARE-BASED PYRAMID NET
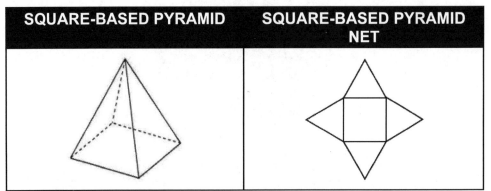

TRIANGULAR PRISM	TRIANGULAR PRISM NET
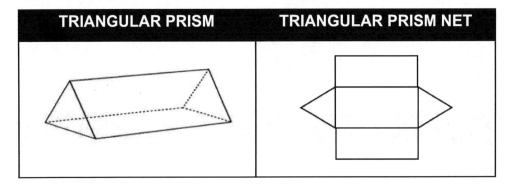

VOLUME OF 3D SHAPES

The **VOLUME** of a shape is the space inside it!

VOLUME OF A CUBE AND CUBOID	VOLUME OF A PRISM
length (l) × width (w) × height (h)	area of the cross section × length (l)

VOLUME OF A CYLINDER	VOLUME OF A PYRAMID
$\pi r^2 h$ Pi × radius² × height (h)	$\frac{1}{3}$ × area of base × perpendicular height

VOLUME OF A CONE	VOLUME OF A SPHERE
$\frac{1}{3}\pi r^2 h$	$\frac{4}{3}\pi r^3$

SURFACE AREA OF 3D SHAPES

The **SURFACE AREA** of a shape is the sum of the areas of ALL the faces.

SURFACE AREA OF A CUBE AND CUBOID	SURFACE AREA OF A CYLINDER
Find the area of each face and then add them together.	$2\pi r^2 + 2\pi rh$

SURFACE AREA OF A PYRAMID	SURFACE AREA OF A CONE
Add the area of the base to the sum of the areas of the triangular faces.	$\pi r^2 + 2\pi rl$

SURFACE AREA OF A SPHERE
$4\pi r^2$

PLANS AND ELEVATIONS OF 3D SHAPES

PLANS and **ELEVATIONS** are 2D drawings of 3D shapes.

A **PLAN** is a drawing to scale which shows the shape as if you were looking directly down on it.

An **ELEVATION** is the view of the shape from the front or the side.

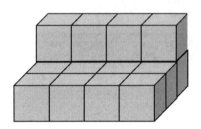

FRONT ELEVATION　　　　**SIDE ELEVATION**　　　　**PLAN**

EXERCISE 4

1. If the statement is true, put a ✓ in the box. If the statement is false, put a ✗ in the box.

   a) Every 3D shape has only one net.

   b) A prism is a 3D shape where the two end faces are the same.

   c) A square-based pyramid has one square face and four triangular faces.

   d) The corners of a shape are also called vertices.

2. Find the surface area of the following shapes:

   a) SQUARE-BASED PYRAMID

   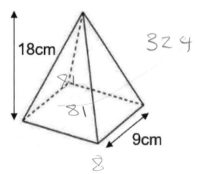

   18cm

   324

   81

   81

   8

   9cm

WORK OUT THE SURFACE AREA

   405 cm²

   ✓

   112 + 56 + 196 =

   b) CUBOID

   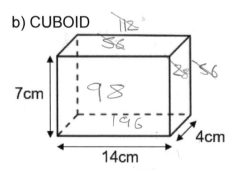

   112

   56

   28 56

   7cm

   98

   196

   4cm

   14cm

WORK OUT THE SURFACE AREA

   86 112
       56
      196

   344 x —

   364 ✓

c) TRIANGULAR PRISM

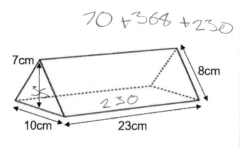

$70 + 368 + 230$

230

7cm 8cm

10cm 23cm

WORK OUT THE SURFACE AREA

668 ✓

3. For the following 3D shape, draw its net.

a) PENTAGONAL PRISM

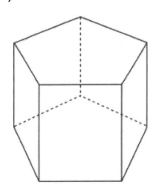

PENTAGONAL PRISM NET

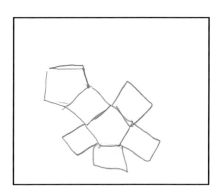

b) CUBE

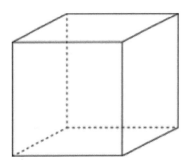

CUBE NET

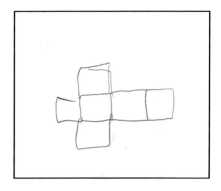

c) TRIANGULAR PRISM   **TRIANGULAR PRISM NET**

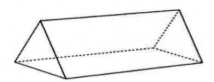

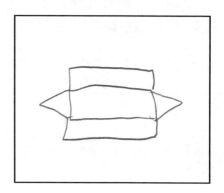

Interesting Facts!

1) *Did you know that the oldest Egyptian pyramid is believed to be the Pyramid of Djoser, which was built during the 27th Century BC?*

2) *Did you know that each side of a standard size Rubix Cube is 5.7 centimetres? Can you work out the total area of this cubed toy?*

3) *Did you know that the shape for The Shard was built with a square-based pyramid in mind?*

26/02/24

CIRCLES, SECTORS, AND ARCS

When it comes to circles, there are a lot of tricky words to get your head around!

RADIUS, DIAMETER, AND CIRCUMFERENCE

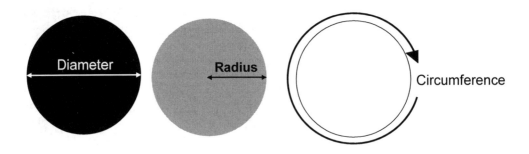

DIAMETER

The distance running right through the centre of the circle, from one side of the circle, to the other. This is twice the size of the radius.

RADIUS

The radius is half the length of the diameter.

Starting from the middle of the circle, the radius reaches the edge of the circle.

CIRCUMFERENCE

The circumference is the outer edge of a circle. Circumference = π × diameter.

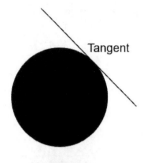

Tangent

TANGENT

A tangent is a straight line which touches the outer side of the circle.

Chord

CHORD

A chord is a straight line drawn across the inside of a circle, but DOES NOT run through the centre.

Sector

SECTOR

A sector is like a 'piece' or 'slice'. Using the mid-point of the circle, create two straight lines which reach the edge of the circle. Sector area = angle ÷ 360° × πr^2.

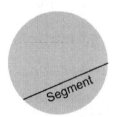

Segment

SEGMENT

A segment is the area you get when you draw a chord. The chord is the line, whereas the segment is the area in that chord.

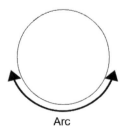

Arc

ARC

An arc is part of the circumference of the circle. Arc length = angle ÷ 360° × πd.

To work out the **AREA** of a circle, you should use the following formula:

Area of a circle = πr^2

EXERCISE 5

1. Match the circle terms with the correct description.

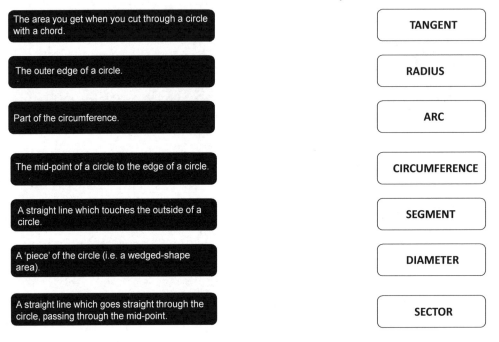

The area you get when you cut through a circle with a chord.		TANGENT
The outer edge of a circle.		RADIUS
Part of the circumference.		ARC
The mid-point of a circle to the edge of a circle.		CIRCUMFERENCE
A straight line which touches the outside of a circle.		SEGMENT
A 'piece' of the circle (i.e. a wedged-shape area).		DIAMETER
A straight line which goes straight through the circle, passing through the mid-point.		SECTOR

2. Below is a circle. Find the circumference and the area. Give your answer to 2 dp.

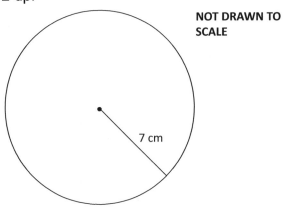

NOT DRAWN TO SCALE

7 cm

3. Below is a semi-circle which has a diameter of 14 cm.

    Work out the perimeter of the semi-circle. Give your answer to 2 dp.

NOT DRAWN TO SCALE

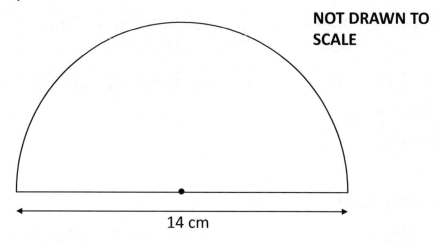

14 cm

4. A circle has a radius of 20 cm. Work out the area of the circle in terms of π.

5. Find the shaded area. Write your answer to 1 decimal place.

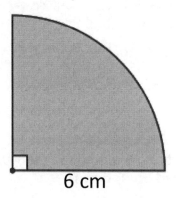

6 cm

Interesting Fact!

1) Did you know that the Plaza de Toroz Las Ventas has an arena with a diameter of 60 metres?

Fact!

TRANSFORMATIONS AND ENLARGEMENTS

You need to learn the four TRANSFORMATIONS when it comes to looking at shapes.

The four transformations that you need to know are:

1. Translations

2. Rotations

3. Reflections

4. Enlargements

TRANSLATIONS

When we talk about translating shapes, this basically means **SLIDING** the shape into a new position.

Translations are very easy to understand if you know how the shape has been moved. That is why we must **ALWAYS** say how far along and how far up (or down) the shape has moved.

We describe the movement of the shape using **VECTORS**.

When describing the movement, you will:

1. First describe the movement on the x axis (how many spaces the shape has moved left or right).

2. And then, describe the movement on the y axis (how many spaces the shape has moved up or down).

EXAMPLE

Take a look at the following grid. Triangles A, B and C have all been translated. But, we need to understand how each shape has moved across the page; and to do this we will use vectors.

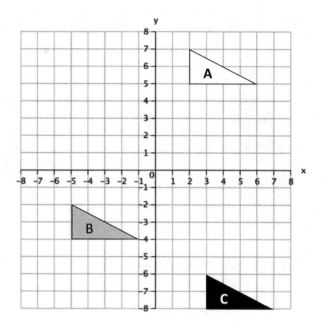

Step 1 = place a black dot on one of the corners on triangle A. Whichever corner of the triangle you have marked, do the same for triangles B and C.

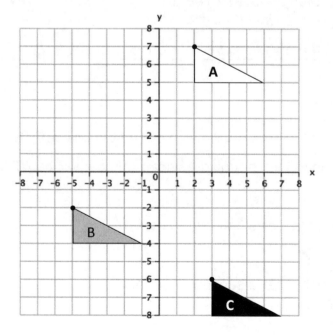

Step 2 = next, work out how triangle A translates to triangle B.

- Using the dotted corner on triangle A, first work out how the triangle has moved sideways.

    The triangle has moved 7 spaces to the left (which means the vector would be −7).

- Next, work out how the triangle has moved up or down.

    The triangle has moved 9 spaces downwards (which means the vector would be −9).

- So the translation by vector from A to B is $\begin{pmatrix} -7 \\ -9 \end{pmatrix}$

Step 3 = next, work out how triangle B translates to triangle C.

- Using the dotted corner on triangle B, first work out how the triangle has moved sideways.

    The triangle has moved 8 spaces to the right (which means the vector would be 8).

- Next, work out how the triangle has moved up or down.

    The triangle has moved 4 spaces downwards (which means the vector would be −4).

- So, the translation by vector from B to C is $\begin{pmatrix} 8 \\ -4 \end{pmatrix}$

REMEMBER

- Moving to the right or up – vector number will be **POSITIVE**.

- Moving to the left or down – vector number will be **NEGATIVE**.

- Describe the x axis first (right or left)

- Describe the y axis second (up or down)

ROTATIONS

Another way you can transform a shape is by **ROTATION.**

When describing a rotation, you will need to know:

1. The direction of rotation (clockwise or anti-clockwise).

2. The angle of rotation (90° or 180°).

3. The centre of rotation.

EXAMPLE

Take a look at the following grid. Triangle A has been rotated to form triangle B.

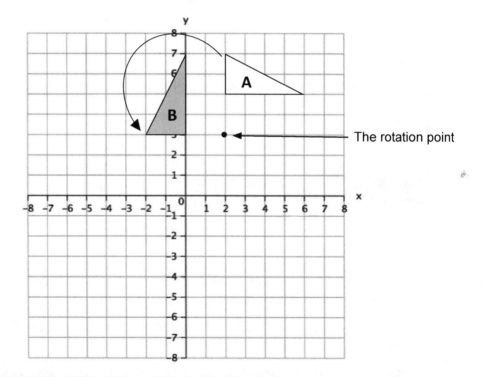

The rotation point

In the above diagram, triangle A has been rotated 90° ANTI-CLOCKWISE.

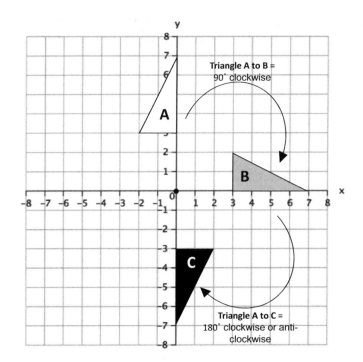

In the above diagram, we are using the centre rotation of (0, 0).

To get from triangle A to triangle B, we have rotated triangle A 90° clockwise.

If you wanted to get from triangle A to triangle C, we can rotate the triangle 180° using the centre rotation vectors. It does not matter whether you go clockwise or anti-clockwise, because you will end up in the same position!

REMEMBER

- Make sure you know the angle of rotation, direction of rotation and/ or the centre of rotation.

- A good way to practice these types of questions is to use **TRACING PAPER**.

- Know the difference between clockwise and anti-clockwise. Clockwise is the direction you will see the hands of a clock moving around in.

REFLECTIONS

Another transformation is using **REFLECTIONS**.

Think of shape reflections as a way of looking into a mirror. Using a mirror line, the object must appear exactly as it does on the other side.

The mirror line can be placed anywhere on an x and y grid.

EXAMPLE

Take a look at the following grid. Triangles A, B and C have all been reflected using mirror lines.

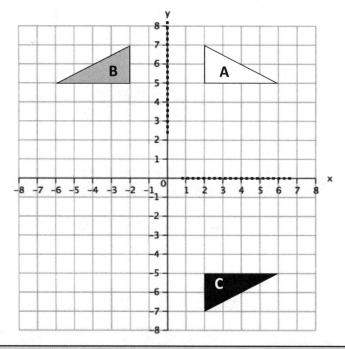

The diagram shows two reflections.

To get from triangle A to triangle B, we have reflected the shape using the y axis.

To get from triangle A to triangle C, we have reflected the shape using the x axis.

The dotted black lines represent mirrors!

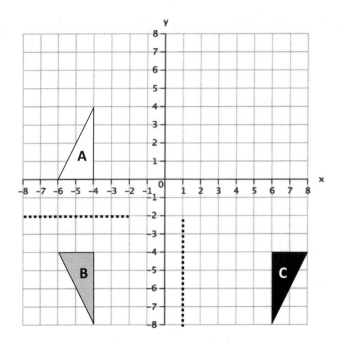

In the diagram above, the mirror line between triangle A and triangle B is $y = -2$.

The mirror line between triangle B and triangle C is $x = 1$.

ENLARGEMENTS

ENLARGEMENTS are a way of transforming the size of a shape.

We can use a **SCALE FACTOR** to work out how the side lengths are changing.

For example, a scale factor of 2 means multiply each side by 2.

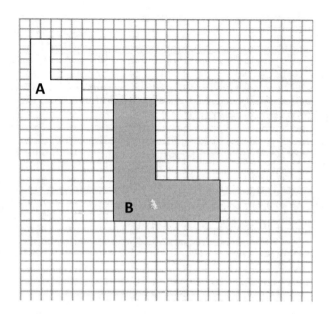

The scale factor of shape A to shape B is 2.

Each side length has been multiplied by 2.

When describing an enlargement, you need to focus on:

1. The scale factor

2. The centre of enlargement.

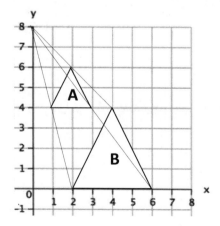

To work out the scale factor:

New length ÷ old length

So the scale factor which transforms triangle A to triangle B is 2.

The centre of enlargement is (0, 8).

To work out the centre of enlargement:

- Draw lines which go through the matching corners of each shape. So, draw a line going through the top corner of triangle A to the top corner of triangle B, and so forth.

- Wherever these lines meet, that is the centre of enlargement.

EXERCISE 6

1. L-shape Y is an enlargement of L-shape X. Work out the scale factor of the enlargement.

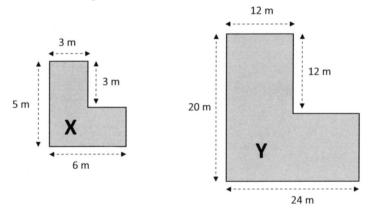

NOT DRAWN TO SCALE

Using shape A, rotate 90° anti-clockwise, and draw the image in the top right quarter of the grid (using the black point as a reference). Label this shape 'B'. Next, translate shape B −7 vertically and +3 horizontally. Draw the shape and label 'C'. Next reflect shape C (using the y axis) into the bottom left quadrant of the grid and label 'D'.

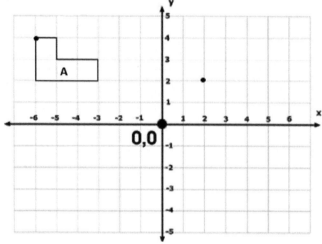

2. Translate shape A using the vectors $\left(\begin{array}{c} -7 \\ -2 \end{array}\right)$. Label the new shape 'B'.

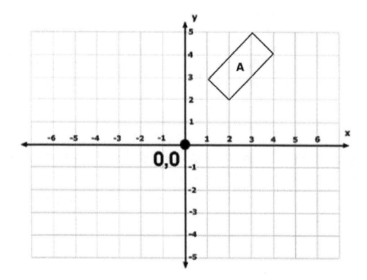

4. Reflect shape A in the y axis. Label this shape 'B'. Using shape B, reflect this using the x axis as the mirror line. Label this shape 'C'.

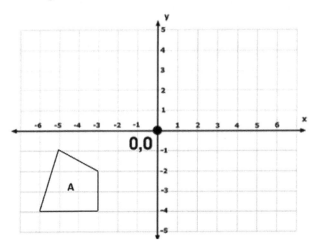

INtereSting FactS!

1) **Did you know that flat mirrors reflect an image as it appears, whereas curved mirrors distort the image?**

Try looking at yourself in the back of a spoon!

2) **Did you know that The Moon is over 380,000 kilometres away from Earth? We know this because of mirrors.**

3) **Did you know that the London Eye completes a full rotation in about 30 minutes?**

Each capsule travels approximately 26 cm per second. That's 0.6 mph!

PYTHAGORAS' THEOREM

Pythagoras' Theorem can be used to find ANY length of a triangle.

PYTHAGORAS' THEOREM FORMULA

$$a^2 + b^2 = c^2$$

When it comes to Pythagoras, there are a few things that you need to be aware of:

- Pythagoras' Theorem can only be applied to **RIGHT-ANGLED TRIANGLES**.

- Two sides of the triangle will always be known, and you will need to work out the third length.

- Make sure that your answer **LOOKS** sensible!

- The longest side of the triangle is called the **HYPOTENUSE**, and this side is always opposite the right angle.

- The hypotenuse is equal to the sum of the squared numbers for the other sides of the triangle.

If the sides of the triangle are labelled a, b and c, then Pythagoras' theorem = $c^2 = a^2 + b^2$

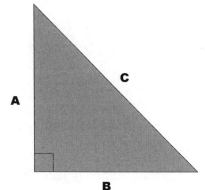

EXAMPLE 1

Find the length BC in the triangle. Write your answer to 2 decimal places.

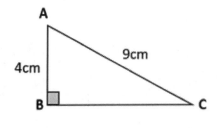

- $BC^2 + 4^2 = 9^2$
- $BC^2 + 16 = 81$
- $BC^2 = 81 - 16 = 65$
- $AB = \sqrt{65} = 8.0622$ cm
- To 2 decimal places = 8.06 cm

EXAMPLE 2

Find the length BC in the triangle. Write your answer to 1 decimal place.

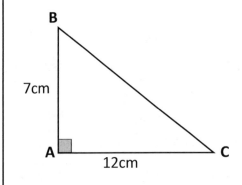

BC = hypotenuse

- $7^2 + 12^2 = BC^2$
- $49 + 144 = 193$
- $193 = BC^2$
- $BC = \sqrt{193} = 13.892$ cm
- To 1 decimal place = 13.9 cm

Key things to remember:

- If you are trying to find the longest side, you will ADD the two squared numbers.

- If you are trying to find one of the shorter sides, you will SUBTRACT the smaller one from the larger one.

- Square the two numbers you are given. There is a squared button on a calculator!

x^2

- Remember to find the square root! There is a squared root button on a calculator!

DETERMINING RIGHT-ANGLES

Using Pythagoras' theorem, you can also work out whether or not a triangle contains a right-angle.

The best way to learn this is through example:

<u>Question</u>

Does the triangle ABC contain a right-angle?

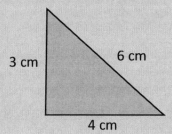

- $3^2 + 4^2 = 9 + 16 = 25$

- The longest side of the triangle is 6cm.

- $6^2 = 36$

- 25 does not equal 36, therefore this triangle does not contain a right angle.

PROBLEM SOLVING

<u>Question</u>

Calculate the length B. Give your answer to 1 decimal place.

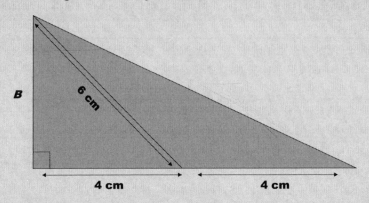

- First work out the calculations for the smaller triangle.

- $c^2 = a^2 + b^2$ $\qquad$ $6^2 = a^2 + 4^2$

- Rearrange the formula to make a^2 the subject.

- $36 - 16 = a^2$

- $20 = a^2$

- $a = \sqrt{20}$ cm

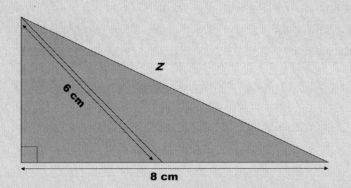

- $c^2 = a^2 + b^2$ $\qquad$ $z^2 = (\sqrt{20})^2 + 8^2$

- $z^2 = 20 + 64 = 84$ $\qquad$ $z^2 = 84$

- $z = \sqrt{84}$ $= 9.2$ cm

EXERCISE 7

1. Work out the length of side A. Give your answer correct to 1dp.

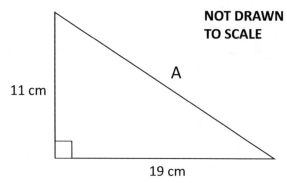

NOT DRAWN
TO SCALE

A

11 cm

19 cm

2. Work out angle X. Write your answer to 3 significant figures.

NOT DRAWN
TO SCALE

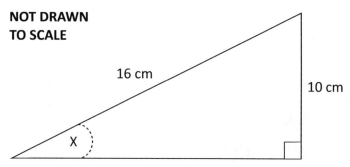

16 cm

10 cm

X

3. Work out the length of AB. Give your answer to 3 significant figures.

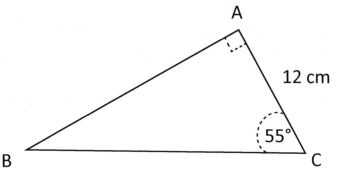

A

12 cm

55°

B   C

4. For the following statements, circle whether they are **true** or **false.**

    a) The correct formula to work out Pythagoras' Theorem is $a^2 + b^2 = c^2$.

    TRUE / FALSE

    b) To find the longest side, you need to subtract the two shorter sides.

    TRUE / FALSE

    c) If the hypotenuse of the triangle is 7.6 cm and the shortest side of the triangle is 3cm, that means the other side of the triangle is 7 cm.

    TRUE / FALSE

    d) Pythagoras' Theorem works with any triangle.

    TRUE / FALSE

5. One of the short sides of a triangle measures 5 cm. The other short side measures 8 cm. Work out the length of the hypotenuse to two decimal places.

Interesting Facts!

1) *Did you know that Pythagoras's cup was credited to philosopher and mathematician, Pythagoras, in an attempt to moderate alcohol intake?*

2) *Did you know that the two smaller angles in a right-angled triangle will ALWAYS add up to 90°?*

Why do you think that is?

TRIGONOMETRY

The hypotenuse = the longest side of the triangle.

The opposite = the opposite side to the angle being used (x)

The adjacent = is the side next to the angle that is not the hypotenuse.

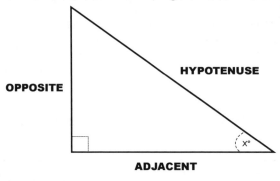

DON'T FORGET:
SOH　CAH　TOA

SOH	CAH	TOA

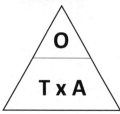

There are three formulas that you need to understand.

$$\text{Sin } x = \frac{Opposite}{Hypotenuse} \qquad \text{Cos } x = \frac{Adjacent}{Hypotenuse} \qquad \text{Tan } x = \frac{Opposite}{Adjacent}$$

Key things to remember:

- When you have a question on trigonometry, you should first look at what two sides you have been given (O,H   A,H or   O,A).

- From that, you will be able to choose which formula you need to use to solve the question (**SOH,   CAH,   TOA**).

- Then using the formula, use the triangles above to show you how to correctly use each formula.

- Cover up what you are trying to find, and do the calculation that is left.

EXAMPLE

Work out the length of the opposite side. Give your answer to 1 decimal place.

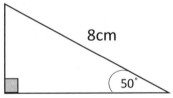

STEP 1

Label the sides.

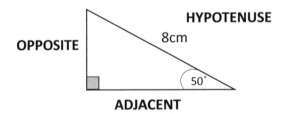

STEP 2

We know the length of the hypotenuse and we need to work out the length of the opposite, so the formula we will use is **SOH.**

STEP 3

We are trying to work out O, so cover it up and do the calculation:

$= \mathbf{s}\text{in } 50° × 8 = 6.12$

To 1 decimal place = 6.1 cm

LEARNING TO CALCULATE AN ANGLE

You can work out the angle of triangles by using the formulas as previously shown.

Let's take a look at an example.

<u>Question</u>

Calculate the angle XYZ. Give your answer to 1 decimal place.

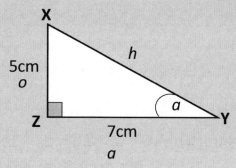

- First, label each side with O, H and A.

- In the triangle, you have been given the lengths of *o* and *a*.

- $\text{Tan } × = \dfrac{o}{a}$

- $\text{Tan } × = \dfrac{5}{7} = 0.714285...$

- Calculate the angle, use the inverse tan button: tan⁻¹:

- $a = 35.5°$

ELEVATION AND DEPRESSION

This is all to do with angles. If someone stands and looks at an object, the **ANGLE OF ELEVATION** is between the line of horizontal sight, and the object.

If someone stands and looks down at an object, the **ANGLE OF DEPRESSION** is between the line of horizontal sight, and the object.

ANGLE OF ELEVATION

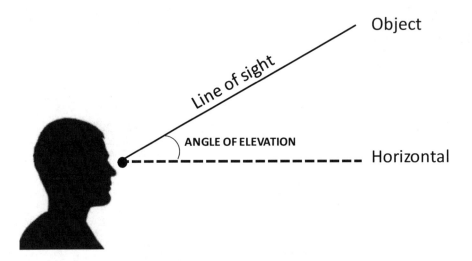

ANGLE OF DEPRESSION

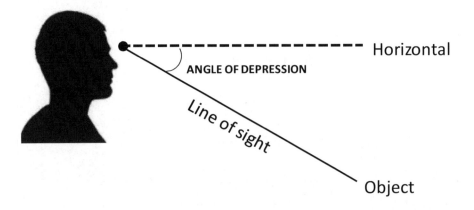

Let's take a look at a sample question involving elevation and depression.

<u>Question</u>

A man who is 1.8 metres tall stands outside a building and looks up. He is standing 30 metres away from the base of the building, and is trying to work out the height of the building.

The angle of elevation to the top of the building is 50°. What is the height of the building? Give your answer to 1 decimal place.

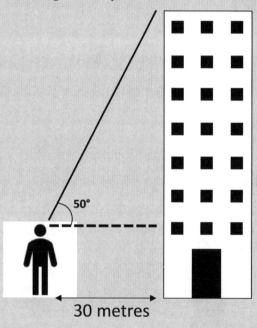

30 metres

- First, you need to label the sides *o*, *a* and *h*.

- In the triangle, we need to calculate the length of *o*.

- $\text{Tan } x = \dfrac{o}{a}$

- $\text{Tan } 50 = \dfrac{o}{30}$

- $o = 30 \times \tan 50$

- 35.8 metres (to 1 d.p.).

- 35.8 + 1.8 (the height of the man) means the height of the building is 37.6 metres.

EXERCISE 8

1. Find the length of AB. Write your answer to 1 decimal place.

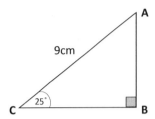

2. Find the length of AC. Write your answer to 1 decimal place.

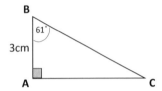

3. From the top of the 12 metres high vertical tree, the person has an angle of depression of 35°. How far away is the person from the base of the tree? Give your answer to 1 decimal place.

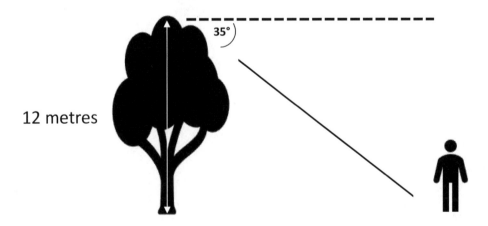

VECTORS

A **VECTOR** describes a movement from one point to another.

A **VECTOR QUANTITY** has both magnitude and direction.

A **SCALAR QUANTITY** only has magnitude.

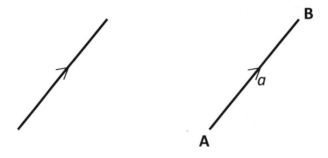

Between Point A and Point B, this can be written as:

$\overrightarrow{AB}$, *a or* <u>*a*</u>.

You can represent vectors by using columns.

For example, $\begin{pmatrix} 1 \\ 5 \end{pmatrix}$

•   This basically says, go along the × axis once, and up the *y* axis five times.

You can also have negative vectors. This will have the same magnitude, but in the opposite direction. You would just put a minus sign in front to show the change in direction (*z*) and (-*z*).

ANSWERS TO CHAPTER 3

EXERCISE 1

1a) An isosceles triangle will always have two angles of the exact same size.

TRUE

b) The angles in a circle add up to 180°.

FALSE

c) An obtuse angle is between 180° and 360°.

FALSE

2) 150°

EXPLANATION:

- Angles in a circle = 360°
- 360 – 90 – 60 – 60 = 150°

3) You should have drawn a triangle with the angles 60°, 40° and 80°. Show your drawing to a friend or family member and get them to measure your triangle.

EXERCISE 2

1) $x = 72$

EXPLANATION:

- 180 – 54 – 54 = 72°

2) A and C

EXPLANATION:

- Only the lines A and C are perpendicular to one another.

EXERCISE 3

1) Your answer should look like this:

Name of shape	No. of sides	Lines of symmetry
Square	4	4
Hexagon	6	6
Octagon	8	8
Heptagon	7	7

2) Your answer should look like this:

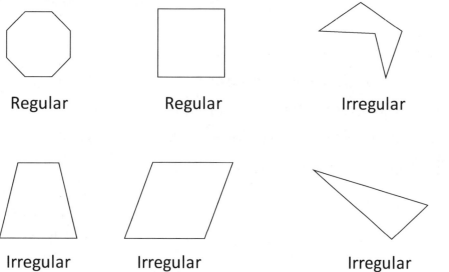

Regular   Regular   Irregular

Irregular   Irregular   Irregular

EXERCISE 4

1a) Every 3D shape has only one net.

FALSE

b) A prism is a 3D shape where the two end faces are the same.

TRUE

c) A square-based pyramid has one square face and four triangular faces.

TRUE

d) The corners of a shape are also called vertices.

TRUE

2a) To work out the area of the square-based pyramid:

- Area of square = 9 × 9 = 81 cm²

- Area of triangle = 4(½ × 18 × 9) = 324 cm²

- So, 81 + 324 = 405 cm²

b) To work out the area of the cuboid:

- Area of top and bottom rectangles = 2(4 × 14) = 112 cm²

- Area of side rectangles = 2(4 × 7) = 56 cm²

- Area of front and back rectangles = 2(14 × 7) = 196 cm²

- So, 112 + 56 + 196 = 364 cm²

c) To work out the area of the triangular prism:

- Area of bottom rectangle = 23 × 10 = 230 cm²
- Area of side rectangles = 2(23 × 8) = 368 cm²
- Area of triangles = 2(½ × 10 × 7) = 70 cm²
- So, 230 + 368 + 70 = 668 cm²

3a) Pentagonal prism net

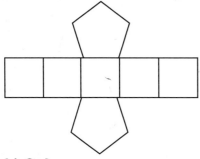

b) Cube

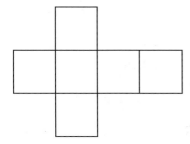

There are lots of different cube nets, so double check your answer!

c)Triangular prism

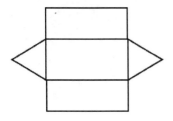

EXERCISE 5

1) Your answer should look like this:

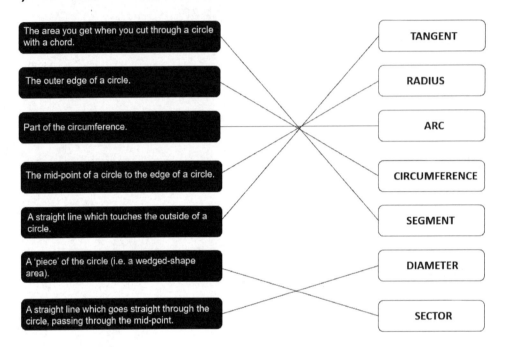

The area you get when you cut through a circle with a chord.	TANGENT
The outer edge of a circle.	RADIUS
Part of the circumference.	ARC
The mid-point of a circle to the edge of a circle.	CIRCUMFERENCE
A straight line which touches the outside of a circle.	SEGMENT
A 'piece' of the circle (i.e. a wedged-shape area).	DIAMETER
A straight line which goes straight through the circle, passing through the mid-point.	SECTOR

2) Circumference = 43.98 cm and Area = 153.94 cm

EXPLANATION:

- Circumference = $\pi \times 14$ = 43.98229...
- Area = $\pi \times 7^2$ = 153.93804...

3) 35.99 cm

EXPLANATION:

- $0.5 \times \pi \times 14 + 14$ = 35.99114

4) 400π cm²

EXPLANATION:

- Area = $\pi \times 20^2 = \pi \times 400 = 400\pi$ cm²

5) 28.3 cm²

EXPLANATION:

- Area of a circle = πr^2
- Quarter of a circle = $(\pi r^2) \div 4$
- Radius = 6 cm
- Area = $(\pi \times 6^2) \div 4 = 36\pi \div 4 = 28.3$ cm² (1 d.p.)

EXERCISE 6

1) 4

EXPLANATION:

- Shape X is 4 times smaller than Shape Y.

2) Your answer should look like this:

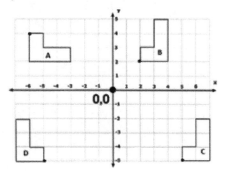

3) Your answer should look like this:

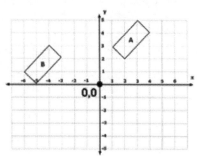

4) Your answer should look like this:

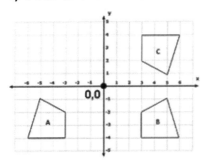

EXERCISE 7

1) 22 cm

EXPLANATION:

$11^2 = 121$

$19^2 = 361$

$121 + 361 = 482$

$\sqrt{482} = 21.95449\ldots$

To one decimal place = 22.0

2) Angle X = 38.7°

EXPLANATION:

Sin X = $^{10}/_{16}$ 0.625

Inv Sin = 38.6821…

To 3 significant figures = 38.7

3) AB = 17.1 cm

EXPLANATION:

tan 55 = AB/12

12 × tan 55 = 17.137

To 3 significant figures = 17.1 cm

4a) The correct formula to work out Pythagoras' Theorem is $a^2 + b^2 = c^2$.

TRUE

b) To find the longest side, you need to subtract the two shorter sides.

FALSE

c) If the hypotenuse of the triangle is 7.6 cm and the shortest side of the triangle is 3 cm, that means the other side of the triangle is 7 cm.

TRUE

d) Pythagoras' Theorem works with any triangle.

FALSE

5) 9.43 cm

- $5^2 + 8^2 = $ long side^2

- $25 + 64 = $ long side^2

- $89 = $ long side^2

- Long side $= \sqrt{89} = 9.433$

- To 2 decimal places $= 9.43$ cm

EXERCISE 8

1) 3.8 cm

EXPLANATION:

- SOH

- $O = S \times H$

- $O = \text{Sin}25° \times 9 = 3.803...$

- To 1 decimal place $= 3.8$ cm

2) 5.4 cm

EXPLANATION:

- AC is opposite to the angle given and AB is adjacent to it.

- 3 × Tan61 = 5.412...

- To 1 decimal place = 5.4 cm

3) 17.1 metres

EXPLANATION:

- In the triangle, the height (o) is known. We need to work out the length of the adjacent (a).

- $\text{Tan} \times = \dfrac{o}{a}$

- $\text{Tan } 35 = \dfrac{12}{y}$

- Rearrange the equation, to make y the subject:

- $y \times \tan 35 = 12$

- $y = \dfrac{12}{tan35}$

- $y = 17.1$ metres

CHAPTER 4
PROBABILITY AND STATISTICS

In this chapter, we will take a look at the following areas:

- Probability and Probability Scales;
- Relative Frequency;
- Mean, Mode, Median and Range;
- Probability Trees;
- Types of Data;
- Bars and Pies;
- Scatter and Lines;
- Frequencies and Tallies;
- Pictograms and Diagrams.

PROBABILITY AND PROBABILITY SCALES

Probability is all about estimating how likely (probable) an event is to happen. It is the 'Maths of Chance'.

Probability is a great way of predicting whether something will happen.

Below we have outlined some 'events' where you'll need to use probability to estimate how likely something is to happen:

- The odds of a coin landing on heads (or tails);
- The odds of a die landing on a 6;
- The odds of it raining in the first week of December.

Below we have created a probability scale to demonstrate how to use them. On the right-hand side, fill in your own example.

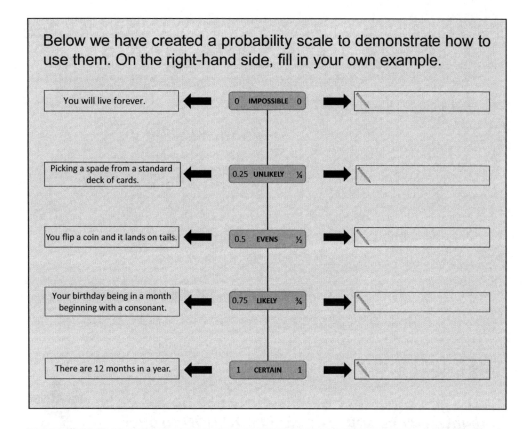

You will live forever.	←	0 IMPOSSIBLE 0	→	
Picking a spade from a standard deck of cards.	←	0.25 UNLIKELY ¼	→	
You flip a coin and it lands on tails.	←	0.5 EVENS ½	→	
Your birthday being in a month beginning with a consonant.	←	0.75 LIKELY ¾	→	
There are 12 months in a year.	←	1 CERTAIN 1	→	

When we think about probability, we are basically saying 'what are the chances?'

<u>We can look at probability in several ways:</u>

- If there is only one possible result, then it will add up to 1.
- If there is a 0.24 chance of something happening, there is a 0.76 chance of it NOT happening $(1 - 0.24 = 0.76)$.
- As you should know by now, ALL probabilities will add up to 1. So, if you know the probability of something that happens, then you can subtract this by 1 to find out the probability of it NOT happening.

$1 - P$ (probability)

EQUAL CHANCE	UNEQUAL CHANCE
The probability of something which has the same level of chance, is known as **'EQUAL PROBABILITY'.**	The probability of something which has different levels of chance, is known as **'UNEQUAL PROBABILITY'.**
We can demonstrate this with two examples.	For example:
1. Throwing a die You have as much chance of landing on an even number as you do an odd number.	If you have a bag of 10 buttons (3 are red, 2 are blue, 1 is orange, and the rest are yellow) you have different chances of picking out different coloured buttons.
2. Tossing a coin You as much chance of the coin landing on heads as it does tails.	**FORMULA** To work out the probability: $$\frac{Number\ of\ ways\ something\ can\ happen}{Total\ number\ of\ possible\ outcomes}$$

Interesting Facts!

1) *Did you know that the chances of being struck by lightning are approximately 300,000 to one?*

2) **Did you know that you have a 16.7% probability of rolling doubles with 2 fair six-sided dice?**

3) **Did you know, in a room of 23 people, there is a 50% chance of two people having the same birthday?**

When it comes to probability, most of the time there will be multiple outcomes.

If you are working with two things, then you will have to work out the multiple outcomes that can occur.

Let's use two coins and see what the possible outcomes are:

HEADS   **HEADS**

HEADS   **TAILS**

TAILS   **HEADS**

TAILS   **TAILS**

WHAT DO WE KNOW FROM THE LAST PAGE?

- There are four possible outcomes:

HH   HT   TH   TT

- The probability of two coins both landing on heads is ¼.
- The probability of two coins both landing on tails is ¼.
- The probability of two coins landing on heads then tails is ¼.
- The probability of two coins landing on tails then heads is ¼.

Below are two spinners. One spinner contains the numbers 1-4, and the other spinner contains the letters A-D.

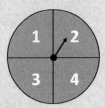 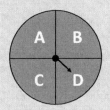

Using a table, we can visualise the probability of two spinners landing on different outcomes.

	A	B	C	D
1	1A	1B	1C	1D
2	2A	2B	2C	2D
3	3A	3B	3C	3D
4	4A	4B	4C	4D

There are 16 possible outcomes (4 × 4). Any number could appear with any letter.

The probability of spinning the number 4 and the letter C is 1 out of 16 (¹⁄₁₆).

$$P(4C) = 1/16$$

EXERCISE 1

1. Below are cards, each with a letter of the word '**PROBABILITY**'.

a) What is the probability that the letter 'Y' is chosen?

b) What is the probability of choosing the letter 'B'?

c) Finish the probability:

P(vowel) =

d) Finish the probability:

P(A-I) =

2. Samuel plays a game of noughts and crosses with his friend, Pete. In the last 6 weeks, Samuel has won 6 games. His chance of winning throughout the games is 0.25.

a) What is Samuel's chance of NOT winning?

b) How many games have they played so far?

c) If Pete had won 50% of the games they have played, how many games have they drawn?

3. Rachel has a bag of buttons. Each button has a number.

6	5	9	4	1	3	6
5	7	9	8	2	5	5
6	9	1	2	9	4	6
3	7	9	5	4	1	2

Rachel picks a button out of a bag at random. What is the probability of picking the following? Simplify your answers.

a) P(odd number) =

b) P(even number) =

c) P(number ≤ 5) =

d) P(number ≥ 5) =

RELATIVE FREQUENCY

**Theoretical probability is what you EXPECT to happen.
Experimental probability is what ACTUALLY happens.**

Relative frequency is determining the likely outcome of something.

Ethan throws a die. He is trying to work out the probability of the die landing on the number 4. Ethan says:

"The probability that the die lands on a 4 is 1 out of 6 (⅙). That means if I throw the die 6 times, I should get exactly one 4."

Theoretically, Ethan is correct. However, if Ethan runs this experiment, this might not be the case. You won't always get exactly one 4.

If Ethan rolls the die 24 times, how many times can Ethan expect the die to land on the number 2?

- If there is a 1 in 6 chance of the die landing on the number 2, this means that for every roll, Ethan has the same chance.

- In 24 rolls, Ethan can expect to roll the number 2 four times.

- Every time Ethan repeats this experiment, his results will of course change!

EXERCISE 2

1. The sides of the spinner are labelled from 1 to 4. The probability of the spinner landing on the number 2 or 3 is given below. The probability of the spinner landing on the number 1 is equal to the probability of landing on the number 4.

Number	1	2	3	4
Probability	x	0.32	0.48	x

The spinner is spun 600 times. Work out an estimate for the number of times that the spinner will land on the number 1.

2. For the following sentences, circle whether you think the statement is certain, likely, evens, unlikely or impossible.

a) Picking a king in a deck of cards.

CERTAIN   LIKELY   EVENS   UNLIKELY   IMPOSSIBLE

b) It will snow in winter.

CERTAIN   LIKELY   EVENS   UNLIKELY   IMPOSSIBLE

c) Pigs will fly.

CERTAIN   LIKELY   EVENS   UNLIKELY   IMPOSSIBLE

INteresting Fact!

1) *Did you know that the odds of a plane crashing are approximately one for every 1.2 million flights?*

Fact!

MEAN, MODE, MEDIAN, AND RANGE

Working out the average helps you understand data more clearly. There are different types of averages.

- Mean;
- Mode;
- Median;
- Range.

HOW TO WORK OUT THE MEAN

The **MEAN** is the most common form of average.
To calculate the mean all you need to do is **ADD UP** all of the numbers, and then **DIVIDE** the sum by how many numbers there are.

MEAN = SUM OF NUMBERS ÷ AMOUNT OF NUMBERS

| 6 | 9 | 12 | 21 | 34 | 27 | 23 | 20 |

To work out the mean:

STEP 1 – Add up all of the numbers.
6 + 9 + 12 + 21 + 34 + 27 + 23 + 20 = 152

STEP 2 – Divide the sum by how many numbers there are.
152 ÷ 8 = 19

HOW TO WORK OUT THE MODE

The **MODE** is the value that occurs the most number of times. This is the **ONLY** average that can have multiple values.

MODE = MOST

| 5 | 7 | 13 | 11 | 13 | 7 | 1 | 13 |

To work out the mode:

STEP 1 – rearrange the numbers in ascending order.
1 5 7 7 11 13 13 13

STEP 2 – What number occurs the most?
The number 13 occurs three times. No other number occurs more. 13 is the mode.

HOW TO WORK OUT THE MEDIAN

The **MEDIAN** is the number in the middle, after you've arranged the numbers in ascending order.

MEDIAN = MIDDLE

| 5 | 7 | 13 | 11 | 13 | 7 | 1 | 13 |

To work out the median:

STEP 1 – rearrange the numbers in ascending order.

1　5　7　7　11　13　13　13

STEP 2 – What number is in the middle?

The numbers 7 and 11 are in the middle. To work out the middle number, add up the numbers and then divide the total by how many numbers there are: 7 + 11 = 18 18 ÷ 2 = 9. So, 9 is the middle number.

HOW TO WORK OUT THE RANGE

The **RANGE** is the difference between the highest value and the lowest value.

To work out the range, subtract the lowest value from the highest value.

HIGHEST VALUE – LOWEST VALUE

| 5 | 7 | 13 | 11 | 13 | 7 | 1 | 13 |

To work out the range:

STEP 1 – subtract the lowest number from the highest number.

13 – 1 = 12

So the range for this set of data is 12.

EXERCISE 3

1. For the following questions, you need to fill in the missing number on the blank cards.

a) If the mean of this set of data is 19, what is the missing number?

MISSING
NUMBER

| 26 | 10 | 12 | 15 | 17 | 22 | 10 | |

b) If the mean and range of this set of data is equal, what is the missing number?

MISSING
NUMBER

| 12 | 12 | 8 | 6 | 6 | 8 | 8 | |

c) If the mean of this set of data is 13, and the range is 19, what are the two missing numbers, assuming that both these numbers are the same value?

MISSING MISSING
NUMBER NUMBER

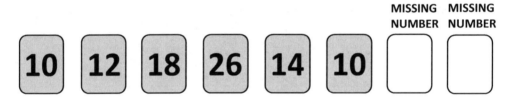

| 10 | 12 | 18 | 26 | 14 | 10 | | |

2. Below are the amounts spent in the last week.

£15.50	£0.50
£4.00	£11.50
£2.50	£30.50
£11.50	£40.00
£25.00	£20.50

a) What is the mean amount spent in the last week?

b) What is the mode amount spent in the last week?

c) What is the range amount across the week?

d) What is the median amount spent in the last week?

3. Below are the scores from a Science and History test. Use this information to answer the following questions. Test scores are out of 150. Fill in the table below.

SCIENCE	68	86	142	35	125	116	75	108	86	74
HISTORY	54	85	49	109	67	85	46	95	126	148

	MEAN SCORE	MODE SCORE	MEDIAN SCORE	RANGE SCORE
SCIENCE				
HISTORY				

PROBABILITY TREES

Probability trees, or frequency trees, are a GREAT way to record and organise data using frequencies. This allows you to work out the probabilities.

Let's take a look at an example.

In a dance show, there are 120 dancers in total. 87 of the dancers are female. 58 of the 87 female dancers are under 18. 16 of the male dancers are over 18.

- There are 180 dancers in total. 87 of the dancers are female.

- That means there are 33 male dancers.

- 58 of the 87 female dancers are under 18. That means 29 of the female dancers are over 18.

- 16 of the 33 male dancers are over 18. That means there are 17 under 18 male dancers.

- This is what your probability tree what would look like:

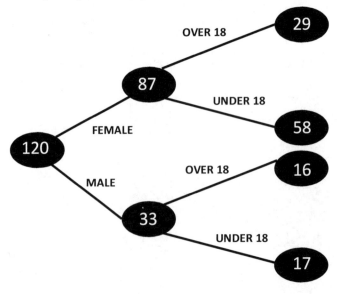

EXERCISE 4

1. In a bag, there are two colour marbles – orange and green. There are 7 orange marbles and 5 green marbles.

    Sammie takes a marble out of the bag at random. She keeps the marble out of the bag.

    She then takes a second marble from the bag. Complete the probability tree diagram.

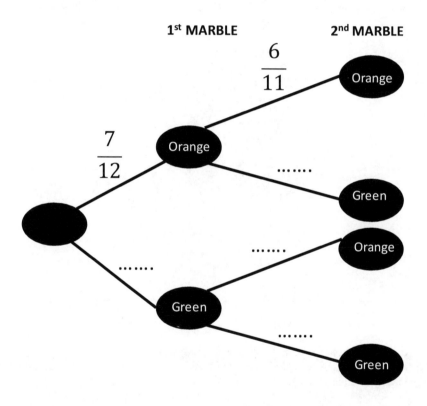

2. There are 14 pens in a box: 9 red pens and 5 blue pens. Marcus takes out a pen. He then takes out another pen. Using a probability tree to help you, work out the probability that both of the pens are red. Write your answer in its simplest form.

TYPES OF DATA

Data is all about COLLECTING INFORMATION.

When you have collected data, you have to know what to do with it. This process of collecting and recording data is the easy part. What you then have to do is **INTERPRET** the data.

Data can either be **PRIMARY** or **SECONDARY**.

PRIMARY DATA	SECONDARY DATA
Primary data is data that YOU have collected.	Secondary data is data that has been collected by SOMEONE ELSE.
Sources of primary data:	Sources of secondary data:
• *Questionnaires* • *Surveys* • *Experiments* • *Observations* • *Interviews* • *Focus groups*	• *Books* • *Articles* • *Newspapers* • *Websites* • *Journals*

Data can either be **QUALITATIVE** or **QUANTITATIVE**.

QUALITATIVE DATA	QUANTITATIVE DATA
Qualitative data is all about using words and detail to describe something.	Quantitative data is all about numbers and statistics.
Qualitative = Quality of description	*Quantitative = Quantities and numbers*
Unlike quantitative data, it doesn't use numbers.	Anything that can be measured using numbers, will use quantitative methods.
For example:	For example:
• *Appearance* • *Texture* • *Taste* • *Smell* • *Scenery* • *Gender*	• *Length* • *Height* • *Weight* • *Area* • *Volume* • *Cost*

Quantitative data can be either **DISCRETE** or **CONTINUOUS**.

DISCRETE DATA	CONTINUOUS DATA
Discrete data works with whole numbers. It is data that can be recorded **EXACTLY.**	Continuous data is data which can take any value (within any range).
For example:	For example:
• *The number of students in a classroom* • *The results of throwing a die* • *Number of goals scored in a football game* • *Number of points in a game of Scrabble*	• *A person's height* • *An age of a person* • *Time taken to finish a race* • *The weight of something*

BARS

One of the easiest ways to display data is through the use of a BAR CHART.

Bars are used on a graph to show the frequency of something (i.e. how many).

Let's take a look at an example. Below is a bar chart showing how many children in each year group had either dogs, cats, fish, or rabbits as pets.

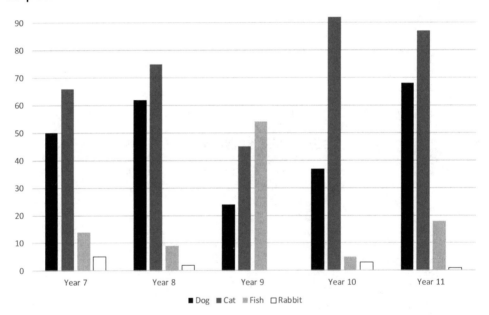

Using the information in the bar chart you can see how many children own each type of pet.

	Dog	Cat	Fish	Rabbit
Year 7	50	66	14	5
Year 8	62	75	9	2
Year 9	24	45	54	0
Year 10	37	92	5	3
Year 11	68	87	18	1

COMPOSITE BAR GRAPHS

Composite bar graphs are a great way to compare data.

A bar chart showing which subject girls and boys preferred.

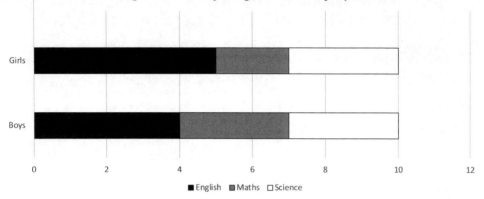

In the above composite bar graph, the following information is displayed:

- 5 girls preferred English, 2 girls preferred Maths and 3 girls preferred Science.

- 4 boys preferred English, 3 boys preferred Maths and 3 boys preferred Science.

PIE CHARTS

A pie chart is a circular chart. The important thing to remember is that there are 360° in a circle.

In order to work out the size of each sector of the pie chart, you need to work out what angle needs to represent each sector.

GRADE	A	B	C	D	F
FREQUENCY	25	10	50	10	5

STEP 1
Add up the total number of people.

$$25 + 10 + 50 + 10 + 5 = 100$$

STEP 2
Next, you will need to work out the fraction of the total for each grade.

- Grade A = $\frac{25}{100}$

- Grade B = $\frac{10}{100}$

- Grade C = $\frac{50}{100}$

- Grade D = $\frac{10}{100}$

- Grade F = $\frac{5}{100}$

STEP 3
Multiply each fraction by 360°.
- Grade A = $25 \div 100 \times 360° = 90°$

- Grade B = $10 \div 100 \times 360° = 36°$

- Grade C = $50 \div 100 \times 360° = 180°$

- Grade D = $10 \div 100 \times 360° = 36°$

- Grade F = $5 \div 100 \times 360° = 18°$

So, you now have the angles of each segment.

Your answer would look something like this:

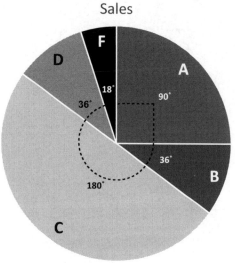

Sales

EXERCISE 5

1. Mrs Alderman has just finished marking exam papers. She had 120 papers to mark in total. The paper is marked out of 150. In order to work out how well students are doing, she wants to put the data she has collected into a pie chart.

GRADE	A	B	C	D	E	F
FREQUENCY	10	15	60	20	10	5

Put this data into a pie chart. The pie has been drawn for you.

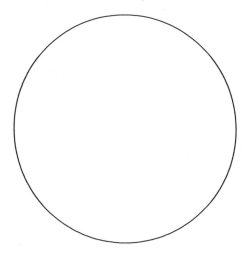

2. Draw a bar chart to represent the different motorway speed limits, based on country.

Belgium	74 mph
Netherlands	62 mph
Luxembourg	75 mph
Spain	80 mph
France	86 mph
Britain	70 mph
Germany	80 mph
Portugal	62 mph

SCATTER

Understanding the correlation!

Scatter graphs are diagrams which analyse multiple sets of data.

They show the relationship between two variables, which makes it easier to analyse the data provided.

The link between the two variables is also called **CORRELATION**.

If the two variables are related in some way, you should be able to draw a **STRAIGHT LINE** through the middle of the points.

This straight line does not have to go through every single point on the scatter graph, but must pass most of the points closely.

This straight line is also known as **'THE LINE OF BEST FIT'**.

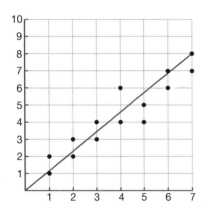

POSITIVE CORRELATION

The points must slant uphill (from left to right). This means that both variables either increase or decrease together.

You can draw a straight line through the plotted data. Dots need to be placed fairly evenly either side of the straight line.

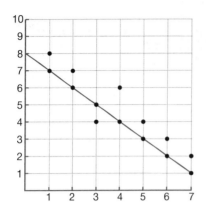

NEGATIVE CORRELATION

This means that the points slope downwards (from left to right). As one variable increases, the other decreases.

You can draw a line of best fit through the plotted data.

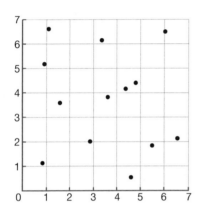

NO CORRELATION

No correlation means that the points are scattered all over the place, and therefore you are unable to draw a line of best fit.

This means that the two variables show no relation.

STRONG POSITIVE CORRELATION

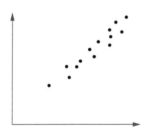

WEAK POSITIVE CORRELATION

STRONG NEGATIVE CORRELATION

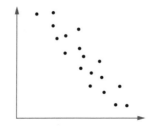

WEAK NEGATIVE CORRELATION

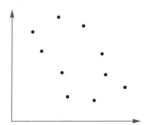

LINE

A line graph is used to represent data over a specific amount of time.

It is often used to show **TRENDS**.

Instead of using bars like a bar chart, a line graph uses lines by plotting on the points and drawing a line through each of these points.

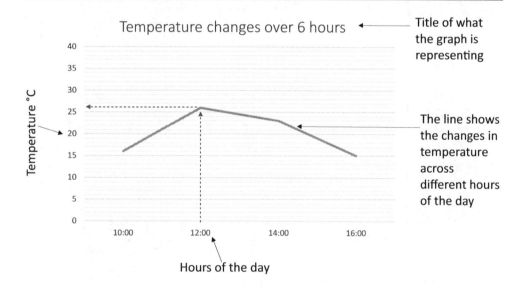

Temperature changes over 6 hours ← Title of what the graph is representing

The line shows the changes in temperature across different hours of the day

Hours of the day

Work out the temperature at 12:00

Step 1 = draw an arrow from 12:00 all the way until you reach the line.
Step 2 = then read along that line and see what number it is.
Step 3 = the answer is 26 °C .

EXERCISE 6

1. The below table shows the results of 10 students' Maths and English scores. Both tests were out of 20.

English	12	18	17	5	9	11	10	18	19
Maths	19	10	4	16	10	14	16	18	20

Plot this data on the scatter graph.

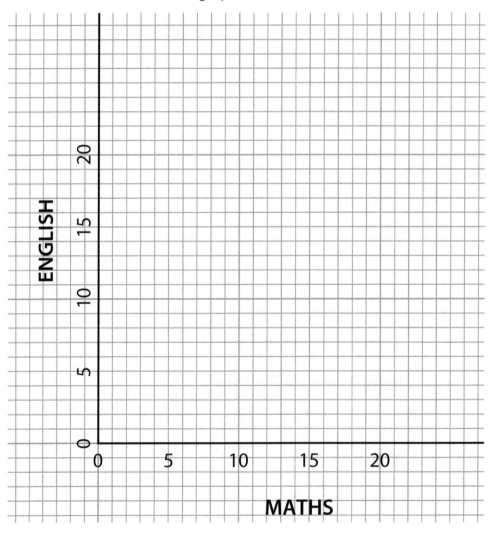

2. Below is a line graph showing the amount of rainfall (in millimetres) across several hours of a day.

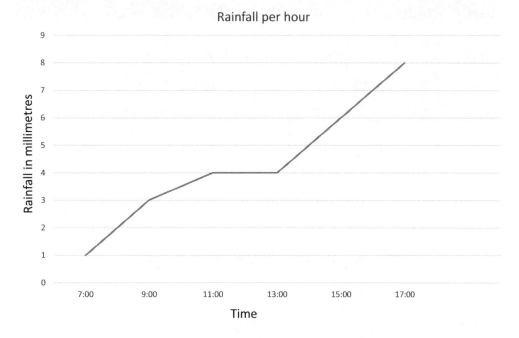

Rainfall per hour

a) Approximately how many millimetres of rain fell at 16:00?

b) Between what times had 4 millimetres of rain fallen?

FREQUENCIES

Frequency basically means:

'THE NUMBER OF TIMES SOMETHING OCCURS'

Using tables is a great way to keep track of data collected.

You will normally have a category row, a tally row (optional), and a frequency row.

This will allow you to quickly see how many are in each category.

CATEGORIES

TRANSPORT	FREQUENCY
Car	22
Train	13
Bus	38
Walk	8
Cycle	17

HOW MANY IN EACH CATEGORY

Sometimes, instead of having individual categories, you will have what are called **GROUPED FREQUENCIES**.

A grouped frequency is data that can be put into classes.

INEQUALITIES often occur in data that doesn't always deal with whole numbers.

INEQUALITIES
The number 5 would be recorded in the top row, but the number 5.1 would be recorded in the second row.

HEIGHT	FREQUENCY
$0 < h \leq 5$	4
$5 < h \leq 10$	10
$10 < h \leq 15$	2
$15 < h \leq 20$	5

$\leq$
This sign means 'equal to or less than'.

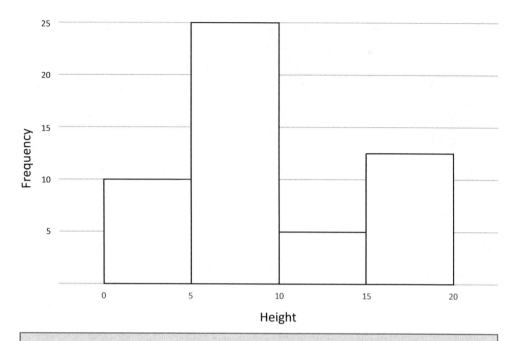

See how the bars in this chart have no gaps.

This is because the groups of classes have no gaps. In simpler terms, because the data deals with whole numbers and inequalities, there cannot be any gaps between the bars, as the data is flowing straight from one class to another.

Instead of drawing bar charts, you can also use **FREQUENCY POLYGONS.**

However, this is slightly trickier and you must remember this rule:

YOU MUST ALWAYS PLOT YOUR DATA AT THE MID-INTERVAL VALUE OF A CLASS/CATEGORY.

HOW TO WORK OUT THE MID-INTERVAL POINT OF A SET OF DATA:

- In your table, you should have your categories and frequencies.

- To work out the mid-interval value, you need to add the upper and lower limits, and then divide that by 2.

The best way for you to understand this more clearly is via example.

EXAMPLE

HEIGHT	$0 \leq h < 5$	$5 \leq h < 10$	$10 \leq h < 15$	$15 \leq h < 20$
Frequency	4	10	2	5
Mid-interval value	2.5	7.5	12.5	17.5

- $0 + 5 = 5$ $5 \div 2 = 2.5$

- $5 + 10 = 15$ $15 \div 2 = 7.5$

- $10 + 15 = 25$ $25 \div 2 = 12.5$

- $15 + 20 = 35$ $35 \div 2 = 17.5$

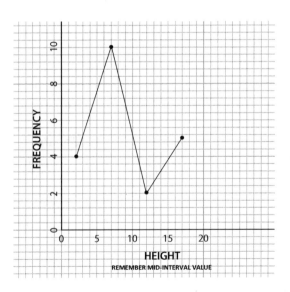

TALLIES

TALLY CHARTS are all about keeping count!

Frequency tables often use tallies to keep track of who chooses what category, before all of the data is added together. The tally part to a frequency graph is often left off recorded data (you can finalise the tallies with a simple 'frequency total'.

Tally marks will look like this:

> Once you get to 4, the next tally mark will cross off the 4 marks (to make 5). This makes it easier to count the totals.

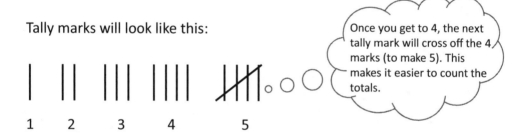

| 1 | 2 | 3 | 4 | 5 |

You can record this information using a tally and frequency graph.

Colours	Tally	Frequency
Pink	JHT JHT JHT III	18
Blue	JHT JHT	10
Red	JHT IIII	9
Orange	JHT II	7
Green	JHT JHT II	12

Remember, FREQUENCY is another word for TOTAL.

EXERCISE 7

1. The table shows information about the lengths (in centimetres) of 20 snakes.

LENGTH (cm)	0 < l ≤ 10	10 < l ≤ 20	20 < l ≤ 30	30 < l ≤ 40	40 < l ≤ 50
Frequency	5	8	3	2	2

Draw a frequency polygon using the data above.

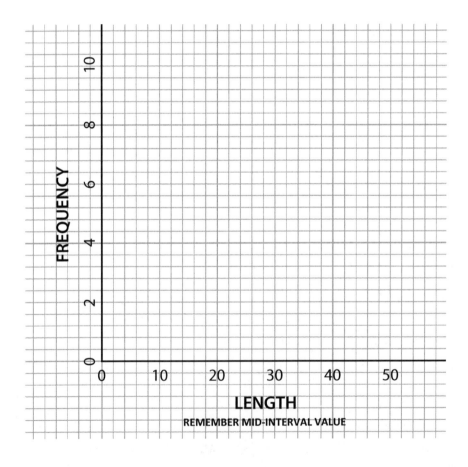

REMEMBER MID-INTERVAL VALUE

2. Below is a list of how 24 children travel to school. Use the data below and organise it in the tally and frequency diagram below. <u>The first tally has been done for you.</u> What is the modal value for the way children travelled to school?

Walk Cycle Walk Bus   Bus   Car   Walk Train Taxi   Car   Walk Bus

Bus   Walk Car   Car   Car   Taxi   Train Walk Walk Bus   Bus   Car

Transport	Tally	Frequency
Walk	|	
Bus		
Car		
Train		
Cycle		
Taxi		
TOTAL	24	24

MODAL VALUE =

3. The following table shows the number of cars that entered a local car park within a 30 minute period.

Number of cars	Frequency	No. of cars x frequency
1	3	
2	11	
3	12	
4	24	
5	24	
6	8	

a) Calculate the mode.

b) Calculate the range.

c) Calculate the median.

PICTOGRAMS

Pictograms use PICTURES to represent data.

In order for a pictogram to work, you must have a KEY.

EXAMPLE

Five people counted the number of balloons they were able to pop in 30 seconds. Here are their results.

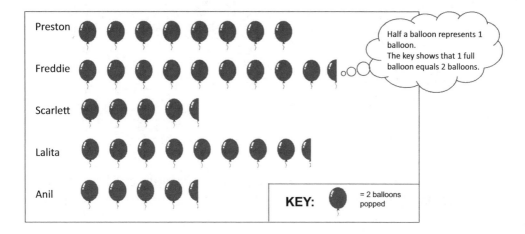

From the key, we can see that 1 picture of a balloon represents 2 balloons.

BOX PLOTS

Box plots can be used to show the minimum, maximum, median, and quartiles of data.

The following information is needed in order to draw a box plot:

- Minimum value;

- Lower quartile;

- Median;

- Upper quartile;

- Maximum value.

EXAMPLE

The lowest score on a Maths test was 53. The highest score was 92. The median was 71. The lower quartile was 56 and the upper quartile was 87.

Represent this data using a box plot.

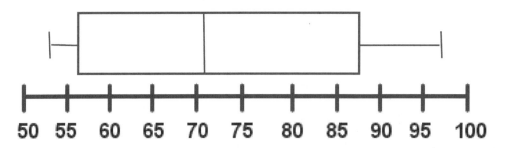

HISTOGRAMS

The important thing to remember about histograms is not the height of each bar, but the AREA.

The area of the bar represents the frequency of the data.

EXAMPLE

The table below shows the age groups of people who learn to play a musical instrument.

Age	Frequency
5-10	18
11-15	5
16-17	6

You now need to find the class width for each of the categories.

Age	Frequency	Class Width
5-10	18	5
11-15	5	4
16-17	6	1

To work out the height of each bar, you need to divide frequency by the class width.

Age	Frequency	Class Width	Frequency Density
5-10	18	5	3.6
11-15	5	4	1.25
16-17	6	1	1

Once you have collected all of the information, you are then able to draw the histogram.

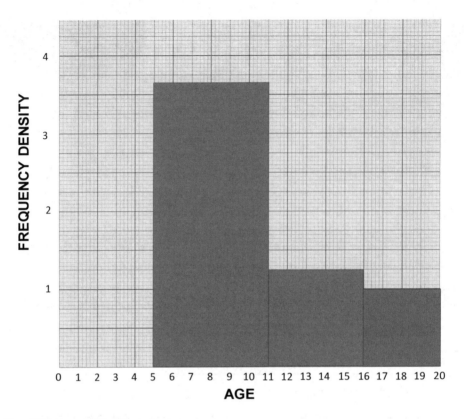

EXERCISE 8

1. The pictogram below shows how many shooting stars Andy saw across 12 months.

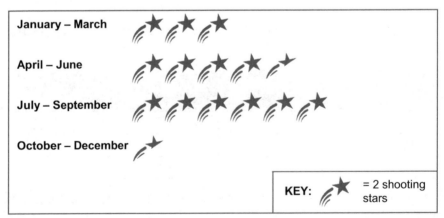

a) How many shooting stars did Andy see between April and June?

b) On average, how many shooting stars did Andy see per month, between January and March?

c) How many shooting stars did Andy see altogether?

d) From April to June and July to September, how many shooting stars were seen?

2. Below is a comparative stem and leaf diagram showing the test scores for both men and women. The test was scored out of 100.

MALE		FEMALE
4	0	6 7 9
5 5 3 2	1	2 3 3 4
9 9 5 3 1	2	0 1
7 7 7 6 1	3	2 3 8 8 9
6 3 3 1 0 0	4	1 1 5 9
2 2	5	2 6 6 6 6
7 1 1	6	0 1
5	7	5 6
4 3 0 0	8	2 8 9
8 1 0	9	1 2 2 6

a) How many people took part in this survey?

b) Calculate the mean test score for women.

c) What is the difference between the range test scores for both men and women?

3. The quickest time for the school's cross country team was 12 minutes. The slowest time for the team was 22 minutes. The median time was 16 minutes. The lower quartile for the team's time was 14 and the upper quartile time was 18 minutes.

Represent this information with a box plot.

4. The below table and histogram shows information about how far students jumped during the annual sports day long jump. The study is out of 136 people.

Mark (n%)	Frequency
$0 < n \leq 2$	20
$2 < n \leq 3$	
$3 < n \leq 5$	50
$5 < n \leq 6$	
$6 < n \leq 9$	15
$9 < n \leq 10$	

Use the table to complete the histogram. Use the histogram to complete the table.

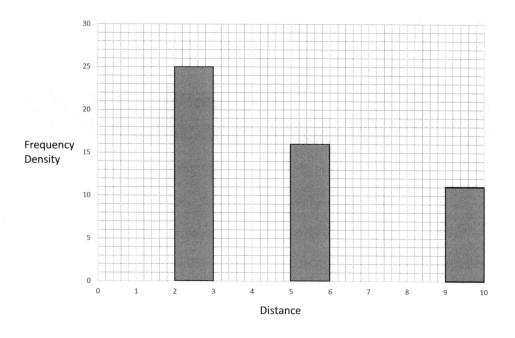

ANSWERS TO CHAPTER 4

EXERCISE I

1a) 1 out of 11 OR $\frac{1}{11}$

b) 2 out of 11 OR $\frac{2}{11}$

c) P(vowel) = $\frac{4}{11}$

d) P(A-I) = $\frac{5}{11}$

2a) 0.75

b) 24

EXPLANATION:

- $6 \div 0.25$

c) 6

EXPLANATION:

- 24 games in total. Pete won half (12). Samuel has won 0.25 (24 ÷ 100 × 25 = 6). So 24 − 12 − 6 = 6. So they drew 6 games.

3a) P(odd number) = $\frac{17}{28}$

b) P(even number) = $\frac{11}{28}$ or $\frac{6}{14}$ or $\frac{3}{7}$

c) P(number ≤ 5) = $\frac{16}{28}$ or $\frac{8}{14}$ or $\frac{4}{7}$

d) P(number ≥ 5) = $\frac{17}{28}$

EXERCISE 2

1) 60

EXPLANATION:

- $0.32 + 0.48 = 0.80$
- $1 - 0.80 = 0.20$
- $0.20 \div 2$ (1 and 4) $= 0.10$
- $600 \times 0.10 = 60$

2a) Unlikely

b) Likely

c) Impossible

EXERCISE 3

1a) 40

b) 4

c) 7 and 7

2a) £16.15

b) £11.50

c) £39.50

d) £13.50

3) Your answer should look like this:

	MEAN SCORE	MODE SCORE	MEDIAN SCORE	RANGE SCORE
SCIENCE	91.5	86	86	107
HISTORY	86.4	85	85	102

EXERCISE 4

1) Your probability tree should look like this:

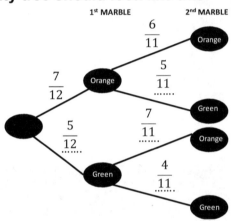

2) $\dfrac{39}{91}$

EXPLANATION:

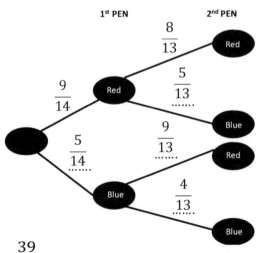

$$\frac{9}{14} \times \frac{8}{13} = \frac{72}{182} = \frac{39}{91}$$

EXERCISE 5

1) Your answer should look like this:

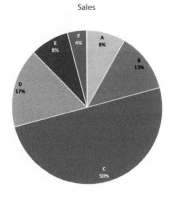

Sales

- $A = 10/120 \times 360 = 30°$
- $B = 15/120 \times 360 = 45°$
- $C = 60/120 \times 360 = 180°$
- $D = 20/120 \times 360 = 60°$
- $E = 10/120 \times 360 = 30°$
- $F = 5/120 \times 360 = 15°$

2) Your answer should look like this:

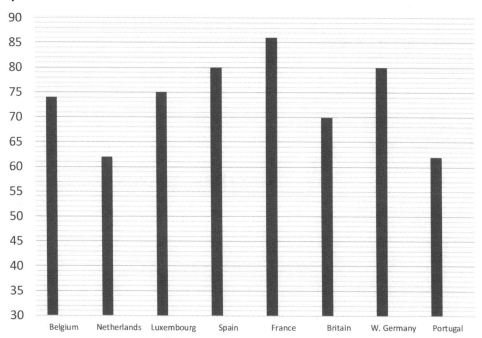

EXERCISE 6

1) Your answer should look like this:

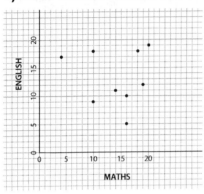

2a) 7 mm

EXPLANATION:

- Find the middle between 15:00 and 17:00 – this will give you 16:00. You should notice that the line on the graph represents 7 mm for this hour.

b) 11:00 – 13:00

EXPLANATION:

- Between these hours, the line on the graph remains on 4 mm.

EXERCISE 7.

1) Your answer should look like this:

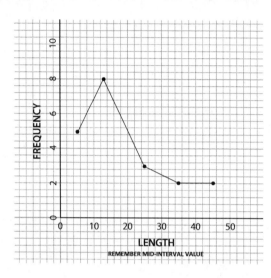

FREQUENCY / LENGTH
REMEMBER MID-INTERVAL VALUE

2) Your answer should look like this:

Transport	Tally	Frequency
Walk	ЖЖ II	7
Bus	ЖЖ I	6
Car	ЖЖ I	6
Train	II	2
Cycle	I	1
Taxi	II	2
TOTAL	24	24

3a) 4 and 5 cars

- Both these categories have the value 24.

b) 6

- Highest value minus the lowest value = 6 – 1 = 5

c) 4

- Frequency total is 82. The middle numbers are 41 and 42. These numbers would occur in the fourth category (number of cars 4). So therefore the median is 4.

EXERCISE 8

1a) 9

EXPLANATION:

- There are four whole shooting stars (equivalent to 8), and one half a star (equivalent to 1). So, 8 + 1 = 9

b) 2

EXPLANATION:

- The average number of shooting stars seen between January and March is 2. If 6 shooting stars were seen across the three months that means 6 ÷ 3 = 2

c) 28

EXPLANATION:

- Andy saw 28 shooting stars in total.

d) 21

EXPLANATION:

- You need to add up all of the shooting stars between the months April – June and July – September.

2a) 68

EXPLANATION:

Add up how many numbers that are in the male AND female sections of the stem and leaf diagram.

b) 48.5

EXPLANATION:

- Add up all of the numbers for the female section, and then divide it by how many numbers there are. Remember that the test scores need to be added based on the STEM and LEAF values.
- Total = 1,649
- 1,649 ÷ 34 (total number of females) = 48.5

c) 4

EXPLANATION:

- Range for women = 96 – 6 = 90
- Range for men = 98 – 4 = 94
- So, the difference is 4.

3) Your answer should look like this:

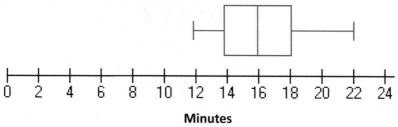

Minutes

4a)

Mark (n%)	Frequency
$0 < n \leq 2$	20
$2 < n \leq 3$	25
$3 < n \leq 5$	50
$5 < n \leq 6$	16
$6 < n \leq 9$	15
$9 < n \leq 10$	11

b)

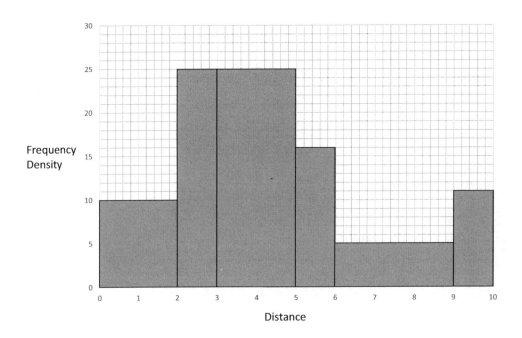

CHAPTER 5
ALGEBRA

In this chapter, we will take a look at the following areas:

- Algebraic Expressions;
- Linear Equations;
- Simultaneous Equations;
- Quadratic Equations;
- Inequalities;
- Sequences.

ALGEBRAIC EXPRESSIONS

When it comes to algebra, letters and/or symbols can be used to represent numbers.

TERM = a number or letter on its own.

- x x^2 $8x^3$

EXPRESSION = an expression is when terms are used alongside operations.

- $3x - 2$ $xy - x$

EQUATION = an equation is a mathematical statement consisting of two equal expressions or terms.

- $3x + 4 = 10$

EXAMPLE

A rectangle has a width of x cm. The height is 4 cm less than the width. Write an expression for the perimeter.

- To work out the perimeter of a rectangle, we need to add up all of the sides.

- Perimeter = $x + x + (x - 4) + (x - 4)$

SIMPLIFYING EXPRESSIONS

Simplifying expressions, also known as collecting "like" terms, allows you to make the expression easier to read.

EXAMPLE

As you can see, the first term does not have an operation shown. However, this means that there is an INVISIBLE + sign.

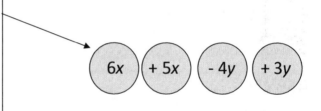

Using the expression in the above example, you can see there are terms that have the letter 'x', and terms that have the letter 'y'.

<u>That means we can simplify the expression as follows:</u>

- The 'x' terms can be collected together $(6x + 5x)$ to give $11x$.

- The 'y' terms can be collected together $(-4y + 3y)$ to give $-1y$.

The easiest way to simplify expressions, is to group each term using brackets:

- $(6x)$ $(+5x)$ $(-4y)$ $(+3y)$

EXPANDING BRACKETS

Multiplying brackets is quite a tricky thing to get your head around.

1. The most important thing to remember is that everything **INSIDE** the bracket should be multiplied by the term (or number) **OUTSIDE** of the bracket.

2. If there is a minus sign **OUTSIDE** of the bracket, that will **REVERSE** all of the signs when multiplying.

EXAMPLE 1

- $3(a + b) + 2(a + b)$

- $3a + 3b + 2a + 2b$

- $5a + 5b$

EXAMPLE 2

- $(y - 1)(3y + 4)$
  $3y^2$

- $(y - 1)(3y + 4)$
  $4y$

- $(y - 1)(3y + 4)$
  $-3y$

- $(y - 1)(3y + 4)$
  -4

- $3y^2 + 4y - 3y - 4$

- $3y^2 + 1y - 4$

You also need to learn how to expand brackets with powers. Powers show how many times a number is multiplied by itself.

EXAMPLE

Expand the bracket $4a^2 (2a^2 + 6a)$

- $4a^2 \times 2a^2 = 8a^4$

- $8a^2 \times 6a = 8 \times 6 = 48a^3$

- $8a^4 + 48a^3$

You will also need to learn how to expand and simplify expressions.

EXAMPLE 1

Expand and simplify $6(a + 4) - 6$

- $6 \times a + 6 \times 4 - 6 = 6a + 24 - 6$

- $6a + 18$

EXAMPLE 2

Expand the bracket $(h + 6) (3h - 2)$

×	$3h$	-2
h	$3h^2$	$-2h$
6	$18h$	-12

- $3h^2 - 2h + 18h - 12$
- $3h^2 + 16h - 12$

FACTORISATION

Factorising is the process of putting brackets back in to expressions.

EXAMPLE 1

Factorise:

$$4y - 8$$

How to factorise:

- First of all, you need to find the highest common factor. This will either be a number or a term.

- The common factor will be placed on the outside of the bracket. The numbers and terms inside the brackets will be multiplied by the outside term.

$4y - 8$

- 4 and 8 are both divisible by 4. So, the number 4 will be placed outside of the brackets.

- Next, you need to work out what you need to multiply by the 4 in order to get the rest of the expression.

$$4(y - 2)$$

If you expand this answer, you should reach the expression we first started with: $4y - 8$.

EXAMPLE 2

Factorise:

$$12ab - 3ac + 6a^2b$$

How to factorise:

- First of all, you need to find the highest common factor. This will either be a number or term.

- The common factor will be placed on the outside of the bracket. The numbers and terms inside the brackets will be multiplied by the outside term.

$12ab - 3ac + 6a^2b$

- The highest common factor of $12ab$, $3ac$ and $6a^2b$ is $3a$.

$$3a(4b - c + 2ab)$$

EXERCISE 1

1. Factorise:

$$64a^2 - 81b^2$$

2. Factorise:

$$49a^2 - 25b^2$$

3. Multiply out:

$$-5(5a^2 - 8b^2)$$

4. Expand and simplify:

$$8(2a + 8) + 4(9a - 3)$$

5. Simplify the following expression:

$$3x^2 + 11x + 4 - 3x + 7$$

6. Simplify the following:

a) $a^7 \times a^9$

b) $m^{11} \div m^7$

LINEAR EQUATIONS

A **LINEAR EQUATION** is an equation that forms a straight line (if you were to plot the results on a grid).

Below are a couple of examples of linear equations:

- $y = 2x + 1$

- $x = 4x - 2$

You can use number machines to write the rules of an equation. The important thing to remember when using this with regards to algebra, is to use BIDMAS.

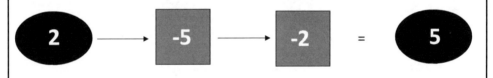

You can work out the value of x by working backwards, and doing the opposite to what the number machine is telling you.

- $x = 5$

SOLVING EQUATIONS

When we think of an equation, we need to think of a balance beam or balancing scale!

Both sides of an equation must BALANCE. Each expression on either side of the equals sign is representing the same value.

To solve an equation, you will need to work out all of the missing values. There may be more than one missing value.

GOLDEN NUGGETS

1. Whatever you do to one side of the equation, you must do to the other side.

2. Often, you will need to get rid of something on one side, to work out the missing value. To get rid of something, you must do the opposite to what it is saying (if the equation uses +, you will −. If the equation uses ÷, you will ×.)

3. You will need to keep getting rid of values, until you are left with one letter.

Sometimes you will need to solve an equation with unknowns on both sides.

EXAMPLE 1

Expand the bracket:

$$8(a + 4) = 24a - 16$$

- $8a + 32 = 24a - 16$
- $32 = 16a - 16$
- $48 = 16a$
- $a = 3$

EXAMPLE 2

Sovle the equation:

$$\frac{6b + 8}{4} = 9.5$$

- This fraction is saying: $6b + 8$ needs to ALL be divided by 4.
- Inverse the operations to solve the equation:

$$\frac{6b + 8}{4} = 9.5 \times 4$$

- $6b + 8 = 38$
- $6b = 30$
- $b = 5$

EXERCISE 2

1. The balance bar is balancing exactly. Using the equation, work out the value of y.

$$8y + 7 \quad = \quad \boxed{119}$$

$y =$

2. If $a = 9$, $b = 3$ and $c = 2$, work out the answer to the equation. Write your answer in the box on the balance bar.

$$2(a + b) \times c \quad = \quad \boxed{}$$

3. Solve the equation:

$$2(4b + 7) - 2b = 3(3b) - 10$$

4. Solve the equation:

$$\frac{4y - 7}{9} = 5$$

5. Expand the following:

a) $-y(3y + 4)$

b) $5y(x - 4a)$

c) $-4(6a^2 - 5x^2)$

SIMULTANEOUS EQUATIONS

The difference between the equations we have previously worked through, and simultaneous equations, is that simultaneous equations require you to work out two unknown values.

To work out the unknown values, you will need to work out two equations at the same time; finding out what the value of x and y is.

EXAMPLE

Solve the simultaneous equations and work out the value of x and y.

$$2x + y = 14$$
$$4x - y = 16$$

How to work it out:

- To try and solve a simultaneous equation, you must try to eliminate one of the unknown values.

- Let's begin by eliminating y (because $+y$ and $-y$ means there is $0\,y$.)

  $6x = 30$

  $x = 5$ $(30 \div 6)$

- Now, using the value of x, you will be able to work out the value of y.

$2x (2 \times 5) + y = 14$

$y = 4$

- You can double check your answers by putting the answer back in to the equation, and seeing if they work for both equations.

FINDING A COMMON COEFFICIENT

A common coefficient is needed in order to work out a simultaneous equations. Some equations will contain commonality, whereas may not.

EXAMPLE

Solve the simultaneous equations and work out the value of x and y.

$$4x + 3y = 55$$

$$3x - 2y = 3$$

How to work it out:

Begin by finding a common coefficient. In this case lets change $3y$ into $6y$. Whatever you multiplied for this, you will need to do for the second equation.

$8x + 6y = 110$

$9x - 6y = 9$

Now we have a common efficient, and we can eliminate this value.

$8x + 9x = 119$

$17x = 119$

$x = 7$

Now you can factor the value of 7 into the equation to work out y.

$(4 \times 7) + 3y = 55$ $28 + 3y = 55$ $3y = 27$ $y = 9$

EXERCISE 3

1. Solve the simultaneous equations and work out the value of a and b.

$$2a + 5b = 33$$

$$a + 3b = 19$$

2. Solve the simultaneous equations and work out the value of a and b.

$$4a - 6b = 0$$

$$6a + 2b = 22$$

3. Solve the simultaneous equations and work out the value of x and y.

$$x + 2y = 22$$

$$-x + 5y = 27$$

4. Solve the simultaneous equations and work out the value of x and y.

$$4x + 2y = 22$$

$$6x - 2y = 28$$

QUADRATIC EQUATIONS

The most general way to write a quadratic equation is like so:

$$ax^2 + bx + c = 0$$

QUADRATIC EQUATIONS contain only terms up to and including x^2. In the above example, you need to remember that a cannot be equal to 0, but the terms b and c can.

QUADRATIC FORMULA

This formula can be used for equations that cannot be factorised. The formula is:

$$\frac{-b \pm \sqrt{b^2 - 4ac}}{2a}$$

Example 2 uses the quadratic formula as a way of explaining it further.

EXAMPLE 1

Solve the following quadratic equation:

$$(x + 9)(x - 4) = 0$$

- The product of $x + 9 = 0$ OR $x - 4 = 0$.
- $x + 9 = 0$
- $x = -9$
- $x - 4 = 0$
- $x = -4$
- So, $x = -9$ or $x = -4$.

EXAMPLE 2

Solve the following equation using the quadratic formula.

$$x^2 + 8x - 10 = 0$$

- $a = 1 \quad b = 8 \quad c = -10$

$$X = \frac{(-8) \pm \sqrt{8^2 - 4 \times 1 \times (-10)}}{2a}$$

$$X = \frac{(-8) \pm \sqrt{64+40}}{2a}$$

$$X = \frac{(-8) \pm \sqrt{104}}{2a}$$

$$X = \frac{(-8) + \sqrt{104}}{2a} = 1.10 \text{ (2 d.p.)}$$

$$X = \frac{(-8) - \sqrt{104}}{2a} = \text{-9.10 (2 d.p.)}$$

EXERCISE 4

1. Solve the following quadratic equation:

$$(x + 27)(x - 3) = 0$$

2. Show how you would factorise the following quadratic equation:

$$x^2 - 4x - 12$$

3. Solve the following quadratic equation:

$$4x^2 + 2x - 2 = 0$$

4. Solve the following quadratic equation:

$$6x^2 - 8 = 32$$

5. Show how you would factorise the following quadratic equation:

$$3x^2 - 4 = 20$$

INEQUALITIES

> As the name suggests, 'inequalities' are terms, expressions, and equations that do not show strictly EQUAL values.

LEARN YOUR INEQUALITIES!

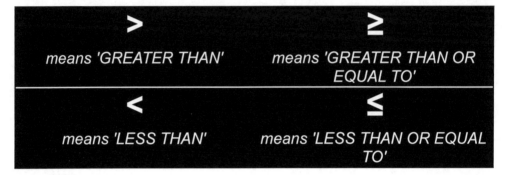

>	≥
means 'GREATER THAN'	*means 'GREATER THAN OR EQUAL TO'*
<	≤
means 'LESS THAN'	*means 'LESS THAN OR EQUAL TO'*

EXAMPLE

$x < 8$

- This means that 'x' is LESS THAN 8.

- The possibilities of the value of x are: 7, 6, 5, 4, 3, 2, 1

$-4 < x \leq 3$

- This means that 'x' is MORE THAN −4. It also means that 'x' is LESS THAN OR EQUAL TO 3.

- The possibilities of the value of x are: −3, −2, −1, 0, 1, 2, 3

A cool way to remember the different symbols...

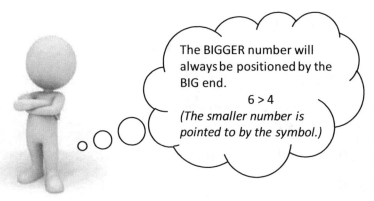

> The BIGGER number will always be positioned by the BIG end.
>
> $6 > 4$
>
> *(The smaller number is pointed to by the symbol.)*

Sometimes, you may be required to rearrange the inequality in order to solve it.

EXAMPLE 1

Solve the inequality:

$$4x + 1 < 37$$

How to work it out:

- In order to solve this inequality, you need to begin by getting the x value on its own.

- We can move the '+1' to the other side, which then becomes '-1'.

  $4x < 36$

- To find x, you now need to divide each side by 4:

  $x < 9$

EXAMPLE 2

Solve the inequality:

$$9y - 1 < 53$$

How to work it out:

- In order to solve this inequality, you need to begin by getting the y value on its own.

- We can move the '−1' to the other side, which then becomes '+1'.

  $9y < 54$

- To find y, you now need to divide each side by 9:

  $y < 6$

When working with inequalities, you can also use number lines to represent the same information.

Drawing a number line is really simple! However, there are a few things that you need to remember.

- If you use > or <, you will need to use an **open circle**. An open circle is used because the number is NOT included.

- If you use ≤ or ≥, you will need to use a **coloured-in circle**. A coloured-in circle is used because the number IS included.

EXAMPLE 1

$-3 < x \leq 2$

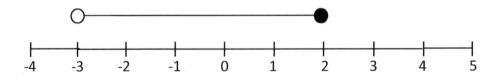

EXAMPLE 2

$-3 \leq x \leq 3$

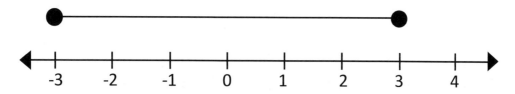

SOLVING INEQUALITIES

Solving inequalities is relatively simple if you have already mastered how to solve equations – it uses the exact same method!

Instead of using an equals sign, you are simply using an inequality sign.

Let us demonstrate this with an example.

EXAMPLE

Solve the inequality:

$$5a + 4 > 11$$

- $5a + 4 > 11$

- You want to move the numbers on one side of the sign and keep the a on the other side.

- $5a > 7$

- $a > 1.4$

- This means that the value of a can be anything that is bigger than (not including) 1.4.

EXERCISE 5

1. Write down all of the possible values of x in the inequality.

$$5 \le x \le 14$$

2. Write down the first six values of n in the inequality.

$$-6 < n$$

3. Draw the following inequality on the number line.

$$-4 < x < 5$$

4. Draw the following inequality on the number line.

$$-3 \le y \le 1$$

5. Based on the number line, write down the inequality for x.

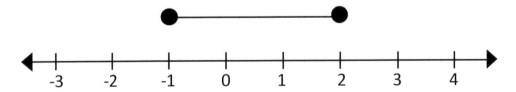

6. Solve the inequality:

$$8(4 - 3x) \le 10$$

SEQUENCES

A number sequence is a sequence of numbers that follow a rule.

There are lots of different number patterns that you should familiarise yourselves with, and these include the following:

- Even and odd numbers;
- Prime numbers;
- Square numbers;
- Cube numbers;
- Triangle numbers;
- Multiples.

LINEAR SEQUENCES

A linear sequence is a number pattern which increases or decreases by the SAME AMOUNT each time.

How to work out the rule of a sequence:

- The secret to working out the rule of a sequence is to work out what you have to do to get from one number to the next.

- Once you think you have found the rule, double check that it works for the rest of the sequence.

- Generally, there are two types of sequences to look out for:

  1. ARITHMETIC SEQUENCES – adding and subtracting the <u>same number</u>.

  2. GEOMETRIC SEQUENCES – multiplying and dividing the <u>same number</u>.

ADDING THE SAME NUMBER

Number sequences may be progressing by <u>adding</u> the <u>same number</u>.

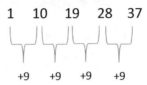

SUBTRACTING THE SAME NUMBER

Number sequences may be progressing by <u>subtracting</u> the <u>same number</u>.

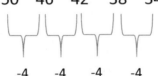

MULTIPLYING OR DIVIDING BY THE SAME NUMBER

Number sequences may be progressing by <u>multiplying</u> or <u>dividing</u> by the <u>same number</u>.

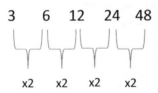

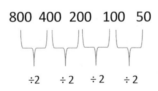

FINDING THE NTH TERM

Sometimes, you may be asked questions on sequences that asks you to find the 100th value.

Of course, you are not going to sit there and work out the values for every number from 1 to 100. You need a quick way to work out the value.

There is a simple method to work out the nth term of a sequence, so long as you know the <u>common difference</u>.

EXAMPLE

Find an expression for the nth term of the following sequence:

$$4 \quad 7 \quad 10 \quad 13 \quad 16$$

<u>How to work it out:</u>

1. First of all, you need to find the common difference. The sequence is progressing by <u>adding 3</u>. So, in the formula you would write $3n$. 'n' is the term you are trying to work out.

n	1	2	3	4	5
term	4	7	10	13	16

2. Next, you need to list the values of $3n$.

3	6	9	12

$(3 + 1) = 4 \qquad (6 + 1) = 7 \qquad (9 + 1) = 10 \qquad (12 + 1) = 13$

3. Work out what you have to do to get from $3n$ to each term. As you can see, you need to <u>add 1</u>.

So the formula is $3n + 1$.

Some questions may ask you whether a value would appear in the sequence.

You can work out whether the value would appear in the sequence by factoring in the value into the sequence and working out the value of n.

If n is a whole number, the value **WOULD** appear in the sequence. If n is a decimal or fraction of a number, the value would **NOT** appear in the sequence.

EXAMPLE

Using the rule $4n + 2$, work out whether the term 22 appears in the sequence.

How to work it out:

1. Let's use the rule and place 22 after the equals sign:

    $4n + 2 = 22$

2. That means $4n = 20$. So you need to work out the value of one n.

    $20 \div 4 = 5$

    $n = 5$

3. The value of n is a whole number, which means that 22 **WOULD** appear in this sequence. 22 is the 5th value of the sequence.

REMEMBER TO USE YOUR COMMON SENSE!

Sometimes, you can work out whether a number is going to appear in a sequence based on all of the other numbers in the sequence.

For example, if all of the values in the sequence are even, that means an odd number is not going to appear in the sequence.

Another example, if all the values end in 2 or 7, that means a number ending in 1 is not going to appear in the sequence.

QUADRATIC SEQUENCES

A quadratic sequence is when the difference between each value is not constant. It becomes a quadratic sequence if the second difference is the same.

The best way to get your head around quadratic sequences is via example.

Take a look at the example below.

EXAMPLE

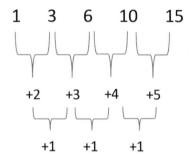

- As you can see, the <u>first difference</u> between each term changes each time.

- However, when looking at the difference, you should realise that these differences are increasing by 1 each time. This is the <u>second difference</u>.

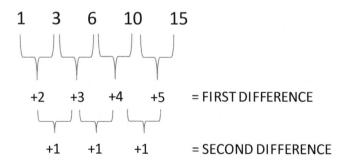

FINDING THE NTH TERM

Finding the nth term of a quadratic sequence is a little bit more tricky than linear sequences.

EXAMPLE

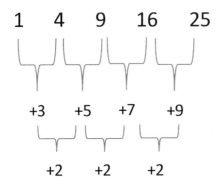

- As you can see, the numbers in the sequence are squared numbers.
- The nth term of this sequence is n^2.

EXERCISE 6

1. Circle all of the prime numbers.

   17   45   49   12   64   91   50   4   5   18   30   15

2. Circle the three squared numbers.

   17   45   49   12   64   91   50   4   5   18   30   15

3. Which two numbers come next in the sequence?

2   4   8   16   32   64

A	B	C	D
126 215	128 256	128 265	182 265

4. Below are four match sticks.

Pattern 1

The pattern continues as follows:

Pattern 1   **Pattern 2**   **Pattern 3**

a) How many match sticks would be in pattern 9?

b) If n represents the number of match sticks, and p represents the pattern number, write the rule to work out how the sequence is progressing.

5. The rule you are given is $7n + 9$.

If n represents the nth term in the sequence, what would the 35th term in the sequence be?

6. Below is a quadratic sequence.

1st term	2nd term	3rd term	4th term	5th term
0	2	6	12	20

a) Write the next 5 terms in this quadratic sequence.

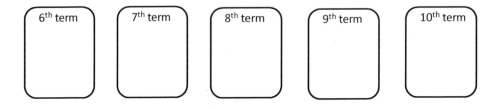

b) Work out the rule to find the nth term in this quadratic sequence.

c) What is the 30th term in this sequence?

ANSWERS TO CHAPTER 5

EXERCISE I

1) $(8a - 9b)(8a + 9b)$

- Both 64 and 81 are square numbers.
- $(8a)^2 + (9b)^2$
- $(8a - 9b)(8a + 9b)$

2) $(7a - 5b)(7a + 5b)$

- Both 49 and 25 are square numbers.
- $(7a)^2 - (5b)^2$
- $(7a - 5b)(7a + 5b)$

3) $-25a^2 + 40b^2$

- $-5 \times 5a^2 = -25a^2$
- $-5 \times -8b^2 = 40b^2$
- $-25a^2 + 40b^2$

4) $52a + 52$

- $16a + 64 + 36a - 12$
- $16a + 36a = 52a$
- $64 - 12 = 52$
- $52a + 52$

5) $3x^2 + 8x + 11$

- $(3x^2)\ (+11x)\ (+4)\ (-3x)\ (+7)$

- $+11x - 3x = +8x$

- $+4 + 7 = +11$

- $3x^2 + 8x + 11$

6a) a^{16}

 b) m^4

EXERCISE 2

1) $y = 14$

- $8y\ (-7) = 119\ (-7)$

- $8y = 112$

- $112 \div 8 = 14$

- $y = 14$

2) 48

- $2(9 + 3) \times 2$

- $2(12) \times 2$

- $24 \times 2 = 48$

3) $b = 8$

- $8b + 14 - 2b = 9b - 10$

- $8b + 24 - 2b = 9b$

- $8b - 2b = 6b$

- $24 = 9b - 6b = 3b$
- $b = 8$

4) $y = 13$

- $9 \times 5 = 45$
- $45 + 7 = 52$
- $52 = (4 \times 13)$
- $y = 13$

5a) $-3y^2 - 4y$

b) $5yx - 20ya$

c) $-24a^2 + 20x^2$

EXERCISE 3

1) $a = 4$ $b = 5$

- $2a + 5b = 33$
- $a + 3b = 19$ $(2a + 6b = 38)$
- $2a + 5b = 33$
- $2a + 6b = 38$

$b = 5$

- $(5 \times 5) + 2a = 33$
- $25 + 2a = 33$
- $33 - 25 = 8$ $(8 \div 2 = 4)$

$a = 4$

2) $a = 3$ $b = 2$

- $4a - 6b = 0$ (x3)
- $6a - 2b = 22$ (x2)
- $12a + 18b = 0$
- $12a + 4b = 44$
- $22b = 44$

$b = 2$

- $4a - (6 \times 2) = 0$
- $4a - 12 = 0$
- $(4 \times 3) - 12 = 0$

$a = 3$

3) $x = 8$ $y = 7$

- $x + 2y = 22$
- $-x + 5y = 27$
- $7y = 49$

$y = 7$

- $(2 \times 7) + x = 22$
- $14 + x = 22$

$x = 8$

4) $x = 5$ $y = 1$

- Eliminate y
- $10x = 50$

$x = 5$

- $(4 \times 5) + 2y = 22$

- $22 + (2 \times 1) = 22$

$y = 1$

EXERCISE 4

1) $x = 3$ **or** $x = -27$

- Begin by simplifying both sides of the equation: $x^2 + 24x - 81 = 0$
- Use quadratic formula with $a = 1$, $b = 24$, $c = -81$

- $$x = \frac{-b \pm \sqrt{b^2 - 4ac}}{2a}$$

$$x = \frac{-24 \pm \sqrt{(24)^2 - 4(1)(-81)}}{2(1)}$$

$$x = \frac{-24 \pm \sqrt{900}}{2}$$

$x = 3$ or $x = -27$

2) $(x + 2)(x - 6)$

- Solve by finding two numbers with a product of -12 and a sum of -4. This is $+2 \times -6$ as this equals -12.

3) $x = \frac{1}{2}$ **or** $x = -1$

If $4x^2 + 2x - 2 = 0$, then $2x^2 + x\, 1 = 0$.

This factorises to $(2x - 1)(x + 1) = 0$.

So solutions are given by $2x - 1 = 0$, and $x + 1 = 0$.

If $2x - 1 = 0$, then $2x = 1$, and therefore $x = \frac{1}{2}$

If $x + 1 = 0$, then $x = -1$.

So the solutions are $x = -1$ and $x = \frac{1}{2}$.

4) $\dfrac{2\sqrt{15}}{3}$

$6x^2 - 8 = 32$

If $6x^2 - 8 = 32$, then $6x^2 = 40$.

This simplifies to $3x^2 = 20$, then $x^2 = {}^{20}\!/_3$.

Therefore $x = \pm \sqrt{({}^{20}\!/_3)} = \sqrt{{}^{60}\!/_3} = 2\sqrt{{}^{15}\!/_3}$.

5) $x = 2\sqrt{2}$ or $x = -2\sqrt{2}$

EXERCISE 5

1) 5, 6, 7, 8, 9, 10, 11, 12, 13, 14

- This means that x is more than or equal to 5, but less than or equal to 14.

- So the possible values of x are: 5, 6, 7, 8, 9, 10, 11, 12, 13, 14

2) −5, −4, −3, −2, −1, 0

This means that n is more than −6.

So, the first 6 values of n are: −5, −4, −3, −2, −1, 0

3)

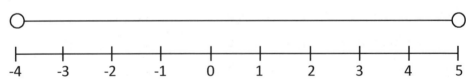

4)

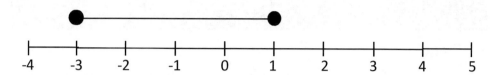

5) $-1 \leq x \leq 2$

6) $x \geq {}^{11}\!/_{12}$

$$\frac{8(4-3x)}{8} \leq \frac{10}{8}$$

$$4 - 3x \leq \frac{5}{4}$$

$$4 - 3x - 4 \leq \frac{5}{4} - 4$$

$$-3x \leq \frac{11}{4} = 3x \geq \frac{11}{4}$$

$$x \geq \frac{11}{12}$$

EXERCISE 6

1) 17 and 5

- Prime numbers are numbers that can only be divided by 1 and itself.

2) 49, 64, 4

- $(7 \times 7) = 49$
- $(8 \times 8) = 64$
- $(2 \times 2) = 4$

3) B = 128, 256

- The pattern sees the previous number doubled.

4a) 28

- The number of match sticks is increasing by 3 each.
- To work out the ninth pattern:

  $9 \times 3 = 27 + 1 = 28$

b) number of match sticks (n) = number pattern (p) × 3 + 1

5) 254

- $7 \times 35 + 9 = 254$

6a)

6th term	7th term	8th term	9th term	10th term
38	51	66	83	102

b) $n^2 + 2$

- The second difference in this pattern is adding 2. That means this sequence has something to do with n^2.

- If we add 2 to n^2, we get each term in the sequence.

c) 902

- We have just worked out that the rule for this sequence is $n^2 + 2$.

- If we want to find the 30th term in the sequence, we would factor this into the rule:

30 × 30 = 900

900 + 2 = 902

CHAPTER 6
SAMPLE PRACTICE
PAPERS

Now that you have gone through the entire Maths curriculum, we thought it best that you practice some sample exam-style questions.

We have provided you some sample pages taken from our GCSE Maths (Higher) book. For full practice papers, as well as detailed answers, please check out Amazon or visit our website:

www.How2Become.com

Answer ALL questions.
Write your answers in the spaces provided.

1. Estimate the answer to the calculation below. You must show your working.

$$\frac{4805 \times 0.213}{5.236 + 4.721}$$

....

....

....

(3 marks)

2. (a) (i) Insert brackets to make this calculation correct.

$$4 \times 12 \div 3 = 16$$

(1 mark)

(ii) Insert brackets to make this calculation correct.

$$2 \times 30 - 14 = 32$$

(1 mark)

(iii) Andy says that $4 \times 3 - 2 \times 7 = -2$

Ryan says the answer to this calculation is 70.

Who is correct, and explain your reasons why.

....

....

....

(2 marks)

3. The diagram below shows the landscape of a field. The area of the landscape is 188 m².

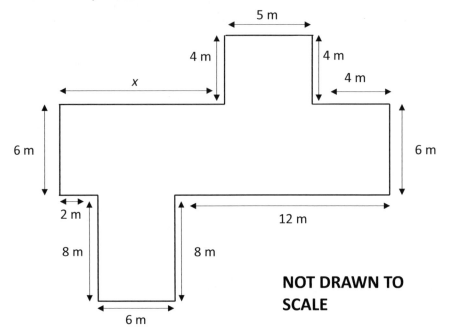

Work out the value of x.

4. (a) Write the following number in standard form:

524,000

....

....

(1 mark)

(b) What is 0.000008 in standard form?

....

....

....

....

(2 marks)

(c) Calculate the following

$(5.5 \times 10^7) - (3.14 \times 10^4)$

Give your answer in standard form.

....

....

....

....

(2 marks)

5. Tessa, Holly and Julie have a bag of counters.

There are 8 orange, 10 yellow and 6 pink counters in the bag.

(a) What is the probability of picking a counter that is either orange or pink?

....

....

(1 mark)

(b) Tessa says, "I don't want any orange counters".

What is the probability of Tessa picking a colour that she wants?

....

....

(1 mark)

(c) What is the fraction of pink counters out of the total of counters in the bag? Give your answer in its simplest form.

....

....

(1 mark)

(d) 6 more counters are added into the bag. These counters are 2 different colours to what's already in the bag. There are now 5 colours in the bag. What is the probability of picking a new colour counter from the bag?

....

....

(1 mark)

6. The below table and histogram shows information about the number of times pupils arrived late to school. The study is out of 136 people.

Mark (n%)	Frequency
$0 < n \le 2$	10
$2 < n \le 3$	18
$3 < n \le 5$	
$5 < n \le 6$	30
$6 < n \le 7$	
$7 < n \le 10$	30

(a) Use the table above to complete the histogram.

(2 marks)

(b) Use the histogram to complete the table.

(2 marks)

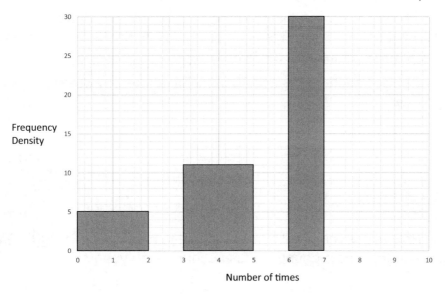

Frequency Density

Number of times

7. David is the Operations Manager of a book publishing company.

   He is conducting self-evaluations with each team member. There are 8 employees who David must spend time with.

   These self-evaluations need to be completed in a 5 hour period, with a short break of 10 minutes between each person. Each person will be self-evaluated individually.

   (a) Work out the maximum amount of time David can spend on each person's self-evaluation.

   ....

   ....

   ....

   ....

   ....

   (3 marks)

   (b) Michael is saving money to buy his first house. Currently, Michael has £3,800 in his bank account. His bank account pays 5% compound interest each year.

   (i) How much money will Michael have after 2 years?

   ....

   ....

   ....

   (1 mark)

   (ii) How many years will it take Michael to reach over £5,000? Only use the whole pounds in his account each year.

   ....

   ....

   (2 marks)

8. (a) Below is a semi-circle which has a diameter of 32 cm.

Work out the perimeter of the semi-circle.

Use the approximation that Pi = 3.1

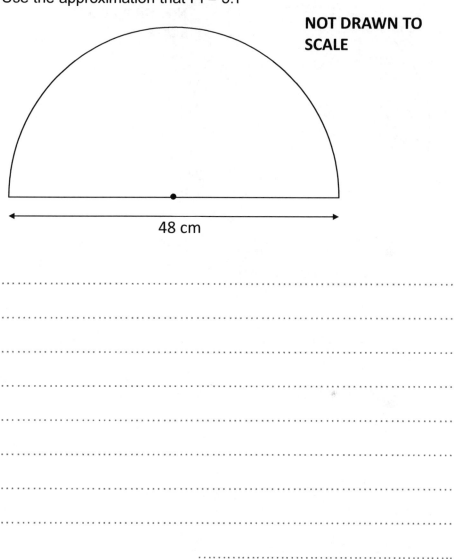

NOT DRAWN TO SCALE

48 cm

....

....

....

....

....

....

....

....

....

(3 marks)

(b) Below is a circle.

Find the circumference and the area. Use the estimation that Pi = 3.1

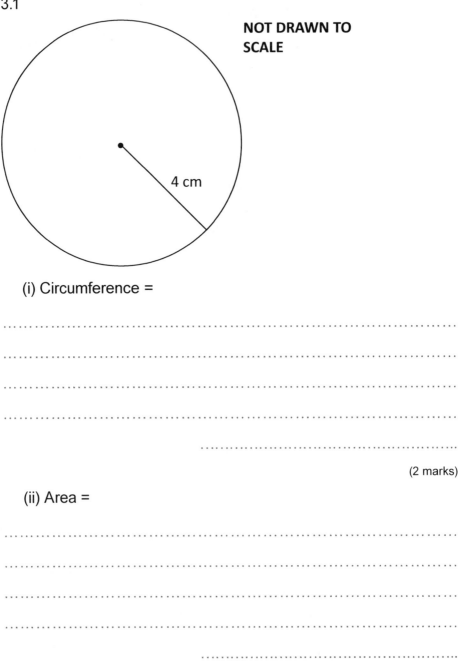

NOT DRAWN TO SCALE

4 cm

(i) Circumference =

....

....

....

....

....

(2 marks)

(ii) Area =

....

....

....

....

....

(2 marks)

9. (a) AB and CD are parallel straight lines.

EF and GH are equal.

Work out the value of x.

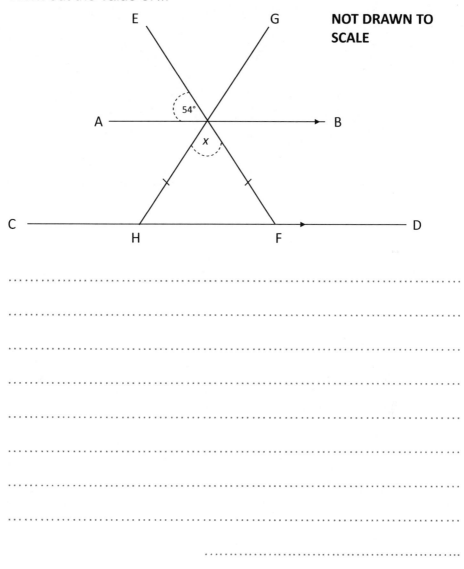

NOT DRAWN TO SCALE

....

....

....

....

....

....

....

....

                    ....

                                                            (3 marks)

(b) Lines AB and CD are parallel.

Lines GH and EF are the same length.

Work out the value of x.

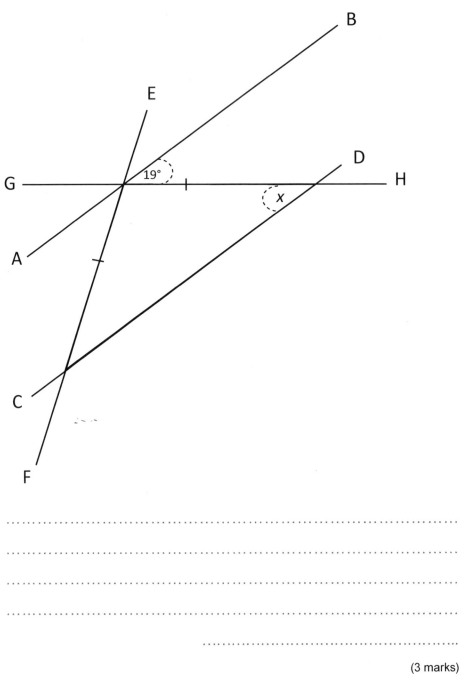

....

....

....

....

....

(3 marks)

10. (a) A scale of a map is 1cm : 30,000cm. A distance is measured as 4 cm on the map.

How many centimetres, metres and kilometres is this equivalent based on the scale of the map?

(i) Centimetres =

....

....

....

(1 mark)

(ii) Metres =

....

....

....

(1 mark)

(iii) Kilometres =

....

....

....

(1 mark)

SET A – PAPER 1

(Non-Calculator)

1. 100	3 marks
Estimations = 5,000 × 0.200 = 1,000	(2 marks for rounding the numbers up).
5.236 + 4.721 = 9.957 = 10	(1 mark for estimation being ± 10).
1,000 ÷ 10 = 100	
Q2. (a) (i) 4 × (12 ÷ 3) = 16 or (4 × 12) ÷ 3 = 16	1 mark
Q2. (a) (ii) 2 × (30 − 14) = 32	1 mark
You need to subtract 30 by 14, before multiplying by 2.	
Q2 (a) (iii) Andy is correct. You need to do the multiplications before subtraction.	2 marks
	(1 mark for correct answer).
4 × 3 = 12	(1 mark for explanation).
2 × 7 = 14	
12 − 14 = -2	
Q3. 11 m	4 marks
12 + 6 + 2 = 20 metres is the total length.	(2 marks for correct answer).
	(2 marks for showing working out).
Therefore 20 − 4 − 5 = 11 (you subtract the lengths you already know, in order to work out the missing length).	

Q4. (a) 5.24×10^5	1 mark
Move the decimal point between the 5 and 7 = 5.24000	
Count how many places the decimal point needs to be moved back to reach its original place = 5.	
So, $524,000 = 5.24 \times 10^5$	
Q4 (b) 8×10^{-6}	2 marks
$0.000008 = 8 \times 0.000001$	(1 mark for correct answer).
8×10^{-6}	(1 mark for showing working out).
Q4 (c) 5.49686×10^7	2 marks
$55,000,000 - 31,400$	(1 mark for correct answer).
$54,968,600$	(1 mark for showing working out).
$= 5.49686 \times 10^7$	
Q5 (a) 14 out of 24 or 14/24 or 7/12.	1 mark
There are 8 orange counters.	
There are 6 pink counters.	
There are 24 counters in total.	
So, $8 + 6 = 14$.	
Q5 (b) 16 out of 24 or 16/24 or 8/12 or 4/6 or 2/3.	1 mark
If Tessa does not want an orange counter, that means the probability of picking a colour she does want = 10 + 6 = 16 out of a total of 24.	
Q5 (c) ¼	1 mark
Number of pink counters = 6 out of 24.	
6/24 in its simplest form 1/4 (both numbers are divisible by 6).	

252 GCSE Maths is Easy (Higher)

Q5 (d) 6 out of 30 or 6/30 or 1/5.	1 mark
If 6 more counters are added, that means there are now 30 counters in total. Which means there are 6 chances of picking a new colour.	
Q6. (a) The bar for (2-3 times) should reach 18. The bar for (5-6 times) should reach 30. The bar for (7-10 times) should reach 10.	2 marks (2 marks for all correct bars. 1 mark for only two of the three bars drawn correctly).
Q6 (b) The first missing gap in the table should be 22. The second missing gap should be 30.	2 marks (1 mark for each correct answer).
Q7 (a) 28.75 minutes	
There are 8 people to perform self-evaluations for. There is a 10 minute interval between each = 70 minutes (1 hour and 10 minutes).	3 marks (1 mark for correct answer) (1 mark for working out the minutes between each individual and subtracting it by the overall total).
The self-evaluations need to be completed within 5 hours = 5 hours – 1 hour and 10 minutes = 3 hours and 50 minutes (230 minutes).	(1 mark for dividing minutes by number of people).
$230 \div 8 = 28.75$	
Q7 (b) (i) £4189.50	
$3,800 \div 100 \times 105 = 3990$	1 mark
$3990 \div 100 \times 105 = 4189.50$	
Q7 (b) (ii) 6 years	
$3,800 \div 100 \times 105 = 3990 = 1$ year	2 marks
$3990 \div 100 \times 105 = 4189.5 = 2$ years	(1 mark for correct answer).
$4189 \div 100 \times 105 = 4398.45 = 3$ years	(1 mark for working out each year).
$4398 \div 100 \times 105 = 4617.90 = 4$ years	
$4617 \div 100 \times 105 = 4847.85 = 5$ years	
$4847 \div 100 \times 105 = 5089.35 = 6$ years	

Q8 (a) 122.4 $0.5 \times 3.1 \times 48 + 48 = 122.4$	3 marks (1 mark for correct answer). (1 mark for working out circumference). (1 mark for showing all working out with no more than one error).
Q8 (b) (i) 24.8 $3.1 \times 8 = 24.8$	2 marks (1 mark for correct answer). (1 mark for showing correct formula for circumference of a circle).
Q8 (b) (ii) 49.6 $3.1 \times 4 \times 4 = 49.6$	2 marks (1 mark for correct answer). (1 mark for correct formula for area of a circle).
Q9 (a) x = 72° $180 - 54 - 54 = 72$	3 marks (1 mark for correct answer) (2 marks for showing workings out of other angles to reach angle x).
Q9 (b) x = 19° Lines AB and CD are parallel. This means the angle of 19° is equivalent to angle x.	3 marks (1 mark for correct answer) (2 marks for showing workings out of other angles to reach angle x).
Q10 (a) (i) 120,000 centimetres $4 \times 30,000 = 120,000$	1 mark
Q10 (a) (ii) 1200 metres $120,000 \div 100 = 1200$	1 mark
Q10 (a) (iii) 1.2 kilometres $1200 \div 100 = 1.2$	1 mark

IMPROVE YOUR MATHEMATICAL ABILITY!

Our How2Become Maths revision guides are the ULTIMATE revision resources to prepare you fully for your Maths GCSE.

Each guide is packed full of examples and practice questions, to ensure that you make the most out of your revision time and can aim to achieve 100%!

FOR MORE INFORMATION ON OUR
GCSE GUIDES, PLEASE CHECK OUT THE
FOLLOWING:

WWW.HOW2BECOME.COM

FURTHER YOUR LEARNING!

How2Become have created these FANTASTIC guides to help you fully prepare for GCSE languages!

Take a look at our 'Achieve 100%' series. Improve your learning with the help of these proven study resources.

WWW.HOW2BECOME.COM

Get Access To

FREE

GCSE

TEST

QUESTIONS

www.MyEducationalTests.co.uk